Public Library Fall River

Appendix No.1, March 1875

Public Library Fall River

Appendix No.1, March 1875

ISBN/EAN: 9783337234171

Printed in Europe, USA, Canada, Australia, Japan

Cover: Foto ©Andreas Hilbeck / pixelio.de

More available books at **www.hansebooks.com**

Appendix No. 1.

FALL RIVER

PUBLIC LIBRARY.

ESTABLISHED 1861.

MARCH, 1875.

BOSTON:
Press of Rand, Avery, and Company.
1875.

Board of Trustees.

THIS work, the *first* of a series of supplements to be issued from time to time, as books may be added to the Library, has been compiled by Mr. George W. Rankin, under the direction of the Board of Trustees. Friends of the Library will confer a favor, if they will kindly communicate to Mr. Rankin the notice of any error they may discover in this list, the authorship of any works treated as anonymous, or the name of any person entered under initials, or under a pseudonyme only.

FALL RIVER, March, 1875.

Special Attention is called to the following Law of the Commonwealth.

"Whoever wilfully and maliciously writes upon, injures, tears, or destroys any book, plate, picture, engraving, or statue, belonging to any law, town, city, or public library, shall be punished by a fine of not less than five dollars, nor more than one thousand dollars, for every such offence"

Days and Hours.

The Library and Reading-Room is open for the delivery of books and periodicals every secular day throughout the year, except those specified in Art. 12, Chap. II., of Rules and Regulations, from 9, A.M., until 9, P.M.

PERSONS ADMITTED TO THE USE OF THE LIBRARY.

Article 1. — All inhabitants of the city of Fall River above the age of twenty-one years, properly identified, who shall sign an obligation to observe all the existing rules and regulations of the Library, and all rules that may be subsequently prescribed by due authority, and all inhabitants of said city between the ages of fourteen and twenty-one years, for whom a parent, guardian, or some responsible person, shall sign an obligation that they will be responsible for said minor's observance of the rules and regulations of the Library, and will make good any injury or loss the Library may sustain from the permission that may be given in consequence of such obligation, shall have free right to take books from the Library so long as they comply strictly with its regulations.

Art. 2. — Any person not included in Article 1 of this chapter may take books from the Library on presenting to the Librarian a written permission signed by the President of the Board and two of the Trustees, such permission designating the time the book may be retained.

Art. 3. — No person shall be allowed more than one volume, and no family of the same household shall be allowed more than three volumes, at any one time. Books may be kept out of the Library fourteen days only; provided always, any book may be renewed once to the same person, but not more than once until it shall have remained in the Library one full Library day. The fine for retention of any volume over the time above specified shall be two cents for every day it is so retained. The provisions of this article are subject to the discretionary power conferred on the Committee on Library and Library Rooms, by Article 5, Chapter I.

Art. 4. — Any book retained two weeks beyond the time prescribed by these regulations shall be sent for by the Librarian; and the expense incurred in obtaining it shall be paid by the person who has so retained it.

Art. 5. — Any book when returned to the Library shall be delivered to the first one who shall afterwards apply for the same; and no book shall be reserved or promised by the Librarian in any case whatever.

Art. 6. — All injuries to books beyond a reasonable wear, and all losses, shall be made good to the satisfaction of the Committee on Library and Library Rooms, by the person liable; and any book not returned within one week after demand for it, made by the Librarian, shall be regarded as lost. If any book be lost, the person for whose use it was taken out shall pay such a sum as the Committee shall determine, or replace the book; or, if it be one of a set, he shall pay the price of a set, and take the remaining volumes to himself, if the Committee on Library and Library Rooms should so determine.

ART. 7. — All books are required to be returned to the Library fourteen days before the annual examination, under penalty of a fine of one dollar; but seasonable public notice shall be given by the Librarian.

ART. 8. — No person having a book from this Library shall lend it to any person not a member of the same household; and no person owing a fine or forfeiture shall receive books from the Library until the same is paid.

ART. 9. — All persons visiting the Library Rooms will be required to demean themselves quietly, and to avoid all unnecessary conversation in the rooms. Any person abusing the privileges of the Library by improper or offensive conduct will be denied admission to the Library Rooms.

ART. 10. — Every person entitled to borrow books out of the Public Library for home use, and desirous so to do, shall receive from the Librarian a printed card, on which the book asked for shall be designated in blanks left for the purpose, by entering the number of the alcove in which it stands, and the number of the book, and if it be a part of a set, then the number of a particular volume, all of which numbers may be easily ascertained from the printed copies of the Catalogue; and this card, which will be presented to the Librarian as the only mode of obtaining any book that may be asked for, will be returned to the owner at once if the book cannot be found; or, if it is found, then as soon as it is duly charged in the borrower's account.

ART. 11. — Books of reference, and those deemed by the Committee on Library and Library Rooms unsuitable for general circulation, shall not be loaned except by an order signed by at least two of the said Committee.

ART. 12. — The Library shall be open for the delivery of books every day, — Sundays, New Year's Day, Washington's Birthday, Fast Day, the Fourth of July, Thanksgiving, and Christmas excepted, — at such hours as shall be determined from time to time by the Trustees.

CATALOGUE.

NOTE.—Authors, subjects, and titles are placed in a single alphabetical arrangement, upon the plan of a dictionary. Where date or place is omitted in the principal entry, which is the one under the author's name, the work is without date or place, or lacks the titlepage. For *full* title find the *author's* name in its proper alphabetical place. If the name is a fictitious one, there will be a reference from it to the real name.

EXPLANATIONS. [] Enclose corrections or explanations.
() Enclose names not usually retained.
* Book cannot leave the Library without permission of the Trustees.

A.

ABBOT (The). *Sir* Walter Scott. 2 v. in 1. 12°. Boston, 1874 . . . 4 . 212

ABBOT, Waldo. Our Sunday school, and how we conduct it. With an introduction by J. S. C. Abbott. 12°. Boston, 1863 . . . . 13 . 877

ABBOTT, Jacob. History of Peter the Great, emperor of Russia. Illustrated. 16°. New York, 1874 . . . . 13 . 878

ABBOTT, John Stevens Cabot. American pioneers and patriots. Life and adventures of rear-admiral John Paul Jones, commonly called Paul Jones. Illustrated. 12°. New York, 1874 . . . . 13 . 109

Captain William Kidd, and others of the pirates or buccaneers who ravaged the seas, the islands, and the continents of America two hundred years ago. Illustrated. 12°. New York, 1874 . . . . 13 . 110

ABINGTON, Mass., History of the town of. Benjamin Hobart. 12°. Boston, 1866 . . . . 13 . 920

ABYSSINIA and its people. With a new map and eight colored illustrations. Ed. by John C. Hotten. Sm. 8°. London, 1868 . . . . 13 . 931

ACROSS America. James F. Rusling. 12°. New York, 1874 . . . . . 13 . 134

ADAMS, Charles F., *editor*. Memoirs of John Quincy Adams, comprising portions of his diary from 1795 to 1848. 3 v. 8°. Philadelphia, 1874. 13 . 1302–4

ADAMS, Charles K. Democracy and monarchy in France. 8°. New York, 1874. 13 . 1356

ADAMS, John Quincy. Memoirs of. Ed. by Charles Francis Adams. 3 v. 8°. Philadelphia, 1874 . . . . 13 . 1302–4

ADAMS, William H. D. The monsters of the deep: and curiosities of ocean life. A book of anecdotes, traditions, and legends. Illustrated. 16°. London, 1875 . . . . 13 . 960

NOTE.—This work is founded on M. Armand Landrin's "Les Monstres Marins," and might not inaptly be described as "Contributions to the Folk-lore of the Sea." It is partly a book of zoölogical descriptions, and partly a collection of illustrations of the "vulgar errors" and "popular superstitions" once entertained in reference to the "Monsters of the deep." The word "Monster" is used in the French sense, as indicating something remarkable, abnormal, or of peculiar interest.

ADAMS, William T. [*Oliver Optic.*] *Army and navy stories.* Illustrated. 6 v. 16°. Boston, 1875.

1. The soldier boy; or, Tom Somers in the army 4.302
2. The young lieutenant; or, the adventures of an army officer 4.303
3. Fighting Joe; or, the fortunes of a staff officer 4.304
4. The sailor boy; or, Jack Somers in the navy 4.305
5. The Yankee middy; or, the adventures of a naval officer 4.306
6. Brave old salt; or, life on the quarter-deck 4.307

Boat club series. Illustrated. 6 v. 16°. Boston, 1875.

1. The boat club; or, the Bunkers of Rippleton 4.308
2. All aboard; or, life on the lake 4.309
3. Now or never; or, the adventures of Bobby Bright 4.310
4. Try again; or, the trials and triumphs of Harry West 4.311
5. Poor and proud; or, the fortunes of Katy Redburn 4.312
6. Little by little; or, the cruise of the Flyaway 4.313

Lake shore series. Illustrated. 6 v. 16°. Boston, 1875.

1. Through by daylight; or, the young engineer of the Lake Shore Railroad 4.314
2. Lightning express; or, the rival academies 4.315
3. On time; or, the young captain of the Ucayga steamer 4.316
4. Switch off; or, the war of the students 4.317
5. Brake up; or, the young peacemakers 4.318
6. Bear and forbear; or, the young skipper of lake Ucayga 4.319

Starry flag series. Illustrated. 6 v. 16°. Boston, 1875.

1. The starry flag; or, the young fisherman of Cape Ann 4.320
2. Freaks of fortune; or, half round the world 4.321
3. Breaking away; or, the fortunes of a student 4.322
4. Seek and find; or, the adventures of a smart boy 4.323
5. Make or break; or, the rich man's daughter 4.324
6. Down the river; or, Buck Bradford and his tyrants 4.325

Upward and onward series. Illustrated. 6 v. 16°. Boston, 1875.

1. Field and forest; or, the fortunes of a farmer 4.326
2. Plane and plank; or, the mishaps of a mechanic 4.327
3. Desk and debit; or, the catastrophes of a clerk 4.328
4. Cringle and cross-tree; or, the sea swashes of a sailor 4.329
5. Bivouac and battle; or, the struggles of a soldier 4.330
6. Sea and shore; or, the tramps of a traveller 4.331

Woodville stories. Illustrated. 6 v. 16°. Boston, 1875.

1. Rich and humble; or, the mission of Bertha Grant 4.332
2. In school and out; or, the conquest of Richard Grant 4.333
3. Watch and wait; or, the young fugitives 4.334
4. Work and win; or, Noddy Newman on a cruise 4.335
5. Hope and have; or, Fanny Grant among the Indians 4.336
6. Haste and waste; or, the young pilot of lake Champlain 4.337

Yacht club series. Illustrated. 5 v. 16°. Boston, 1874, 75.

1. Little Bobtail; or, the wreck of the Penobscot 4.338
2. The yacht club; or, the young boat builder 4.339

ADAMS, William T. *Yacht club series (continued).*
3. Money-maker; or, the victory of the Basilisk . . . . 4 . 340
4. The coming wave; or, the hidden treasure of High Rock . . . . . 4 . 341
5. The Dorcas club; or, our girls afloat . . . . 4 . 342

Young America abroad. First series. Illustrated. 6 v. 16°. Boston, 1875.
1. Outward bound; or, Young America afloat . . . . 4 . 343
2. Shamrock and thistle; or, Young America in Ireland and Scotland . 4 . 344
3. Red cross; or, Young America in England and Wales . . . . 4 . 345
4. Dikes and ditches; or, Young America in Holland and Belgium . . 4 . 346
5. Palace and cottage; or, Young America in France and Switzerland . 4 . 347
6. Down the Rhine; or, Young America in Germany . . . . 4 . 348

Young America abroad. Second Series. Illustrated. 4 v. 16°. Boston, 1873–75.
1. Up the Baltic; or, Young America in Norway, Sweden, and Denmark 4 . 349
2. Northern lands; or, Young America in Russia and Prussia . . . . 4 . 350
3. Cross and crescent; or, Young America in Turkey and Greece . . . 4 . 351
4. Sunny shores; or, Young America in Italy and Austria . . . . . . 4 . 352

The way of the world. A novel. Illustrated. 12°. Boston, 1875 . 4 . 353

ADVENTURES in the land of the behemoth. [Africa.] Jules Verne. Sm. 8°. Boston, 1874. 2 copies . . . . 4 . 1212–13

ADVENTURES in Morocco, and journeys through the oases of Draa and Tafilet. *Dr.* Gerhard Rohlfs. 8°. London, 1874 . . . . 13 . 1351

ADVENTURES of Capt. Blake. W. H. Maxwell. Sm. 8°. London [n. d.]. 4 . 426

ADVENTURES of Capt. O'Sullivan. W. H. Maxwell. Sm. 8°. London [n. d.] . . . . 4 . 427

AFLOAT and ashore. J. F. Cooper. 12°. New York, 1873 . . . . . 4 . 1040

AFLOAT in the forest. M. Reid. 16°. Boston, 1873 . . . . 4 . 1237

AFRICA. DENHAM, D., and CLAPPERTON, H. Narrative of travels and discoveries in Northern and Central Africa in the years 1822–24. 2 v. 8°. London, 1824 . . . . 13 . 1232–33

FORBES, A. G. Geographical exploration and Christian enterprise in Africa. Sm. 8°. London, 1874 . . . . 13 . 1172

GRANT, J. A. A walk across Africa. 8°. Edinburgh and London, 1864 . . . . 13 . 1219

SCHWEINFURTH, G. The heart of Africa. 2 v. Roy. 8°. New York, 1874 . . . . 13 . 1311–12

AFTER the ball, and other poems. Nora Perry. 16°. Boston, 1875 . . 21 . 247

AIKIN, Lucy. Epistles on women, with miscellaneous poems. 12°. Boston, 1810 . . . . 21 . 251

AINSWORTH, William Harrison. Auriol; or, the elixir of life. 16°. London [n. d.] . . . . 4 . 1167

Crichton. 16° London [n. d.] . . . . 4 . 1168

The flitch of bacon. 16°. London [n. d.] . . . . 4 . 1169

Guy Fawkes; or, the gunpowder treason. An historical romance. 16°. London [n. d.] . . . . 4 . 1170

Jack Sheppard. A romance. 16°. London [n. d.] . . . . 4 . 1171

James the second; or, the revolution of 1688. An historical romance. 16°. London [n. d.]. . . . . 4 . 1172

The Lancashire witches. A romance of Pendle forest. 16°. London [n. d.] 4 . 1173

Ainsworth, William Harrison (*continued*).
Mervyn Clitheroe. 16°. London [n. d.] . . . . 4 . 1174
The miser's daughter. A tale. 16°. London [n. d.] . . . . 4 . 1175
Old Saint Paul's. A tale of the plague and the fire. 16°. London [n. d.] . . . . 4 . 1176
Ovingdean grange. A tale of the South Downs. 16°. London [n. d.] 4 . 1177
Rookwood. A romance. 16°. London [n. d.] . . . . 4 . 1178
Saint James; or, the court of Queen Anne. An historical romance. 16°. London [n. d.] . . . . 4 . 1179
The spendthrift. A tale 16°. London [n. d.] . . . . 4 . 1180
The star-chamber. An historical romance. 16°. London [n. d.] . . 4 . 1181
The tower of London. An historical romance. 16°. London [n. d.] 4 . 1182
Windsor Castle. An historical romance. 16°. London [n. d.] . . 4 . 1183
Alcestis. A novel. 16°. New York, 1874 . . . . 4 . 852
Alcott, Louisa May. Aunt Jo's scrap-bag. Vol. 3. 16°. Boston, 1874. 4 . 881
Aldrich, Thomas Bailey. Prudence Palfrey. (A novel). 16°. Boston, 1875 . . . . 4 . 573
Alexander, *Mrs.* Which shall it be? 16°. New York, 1874 . . . . 4 . 853
The wooing o't. 16°. New York, 1873 . . . . 4 . 854
Alger, Horatio, jun. Brave and bold; or, the fortunes of a factory boy. Illustrated. 16°. Boston, 1874 . . . . 4 . 1143
Campaign Series. Illustrated. 3 v. 16°. Boston, 1864–66.
1. Frank's campaign. The farm and the camp . . . . 4 . 1144
2. Paul Prescott's charge . . . . 4 . 1145
3. Charlie Codman's cruise . . . . 4 . 1146

Luck and pluck series. Illustrated. 4 v. 16°. Boston, 1869–72.
1. Luck and pluck; or, John Oakley's inheritance . . . . 4 . 1147
2. Sink or swim; or, Harry Raymond's resolve . . . . 4 . 1148
3. Strong and steady; or, paddle your own canoe . . . . 4 . 1149
4. Strive and succeed; or, the progress of Walter Conrad . . . . 4 . 1150

Luck and pluck. Second series. Illustrated. 3 v. 16°. Boston, 1873–74.
1. Try and trust; or, the story of a bound boy . . . . 4 . 1151
2. Bound to rise; or, Harry Walton's motto . . . . 4 . 1152
3. Risen from the ranks; or, Harry Walton's success . . . . 4 . 1153

Ragged Dick series. Illustrated. 6 v. 16°. Boston, 1868–70.
1. Ragged Dick; or, street-life in New York with the boot-blacks . . . 4 . 1154
2. Fame and fortune; or, the progress of Richard Hunter. 2 copies . 4 . 1155–56
3. Mark the match-boy; or, Richard Hunter's ward . . . . 4 . 1157
4. Rough and ready; or, life among the New York newsboys . . . . 4 . 1158
5. Ben the luggage-boy; or, among the wharves . . . . 4 . 1159
6. Rufus and Rose; or, the fortunes of Rough and ready . . . . 4 . 1160

Tattered Tom series. Illustrated. 4 v. 16°. Boston, 1871–72.
1. Tattered Tom; or, the story of a street Arab . . . . 4 . 1161
2. Paul the peddler; or, the adventures of a young street merchant . . 4 . 1162
3. Phil the fiddler; or, the story of a young street musician . . . . . . 4 . 1163
4. Slow and sure; or, from the street to the shop . . . . 4 . 1164

Tattered Tom. Second series. 16°. Boston, 1874.
Julius: or, the street boy out West. 2 copies . . . . 4 . 1165–66

ALIDE. Emma Lazarus. 12°. Philadelphia, 1874 . . . . 4 . 478
ALL aboard. W. T. Adams. 16°. Boston, 1875 . . . . 4 . 309
ALL in the wrong. T. Hook. 16°. London [n. d.] . . . . 4 . 807
ALLWORTH abbey. E. D. E. N. Southworth. 12°. Philadelphia, 1865 . 4 . 1001
ALONE. M. V. Terhune. 12°. New York, 1874 . . . . 4 . 1101
*ALPINE plants. Ed. by David Wooster. 8°. London, 1874 . . . . . 13 . 1542
ALSACIAN (The) schoolmaster. MM. Erckmann-Chatrian. Sm. 8°. London [n. d] . . . . 4 . 937
AMERICA. SUMNER, CHARLES. Prophetic voices concerning America. 8°. Boston, 1874 . . . . 13 . 1251
AMERICAN currency, History of. W. G. Sumner. 12°. New York, 1874 . 13 . 933
AMERICAN journal of science and arts. Ed. by J. D. Dana, B. Silliman, A. Gray, W. Gibbs, *and others.* 3d series. Vols. 7 and 8. 8°. New Haven, 1874 . . . . 18 . 1462–63
AMERICAN wild-fowl shooting. J. W. Long. 16°. New York, 1874 . . 13 . 1150
AMES, Mary Clemmer. His two wives. 12°. New York, 1875. 2 copies. 4 . 921–22
AMONG the Arabs: adventures in the desert, and sketches of life and character in tent and town. Illustrated. 16°. New York [n. d.] . . . 13 . 966
*ANATOMICAL plates, A series of. Jones Quain, M. D., and W. J. E. Wilson, M.D. 4°. Philadelphia, 1852 . . . . 13 . 1504
ANATOMY of the Invertebrata. C. Th. von Siebold. Trans. from the German with additions and notes by Waldo I. Burnett. 8°. Boston, 1874. 13 . 1305
ANCIENT (The) city. M. D. Fustel de Coulanges. Sm. 8°. Boston, 1874. 13 . 1252
ANCIENT monarchies. George Rawlinson. 3 v. 8°. New York, 1871. 13 . 1326–28
ANDERSEN, Hans Christian. Stories and tales. Illustrated. 12°. New York, 1872 . . . . 4 . 253
ANDREWS, J. N. History of the Sabbath and first day of the week. 12°. Battle Creek, Mich., 1873 . . . . 13 . 1271
ANECDOTE biographies of Thackeray and Dickens. Ed. by R. H. Stoddard. 16°. New York, 1874 . . . . 13 . 971
ANECDOTES of distinguished persons. W. Seward. 4 v. Sm. 8°. London, 1798 . . . . 13 . 1201–4
ANIMAL mechanism. E. J. Marey. Sm. 8°. New York, 1874 . . . . 13 . 1143
ANNE of Geierstein. *Sir* Walter Scott. 2 v. in 1. 12°. Boston, 1873 . 4 . 213
ANTHONY Brade. R. T. S. Lowell. 16°. Boston, 1874. 2 copies. . 4 . 927–28
ANTIQUARY (The). *Sir* W. Scott. 2 v. in 1. 12°. Boston, 1873 . . . 4 . 214
APOSTOLICAL (The) fathers. James Donaldson. Sm. 8°. London, 1875. 13 . 155
*ARCHITECTURE, Gothick, An analysis of. With illustrations. Raphael and J. Arthur Brandon. 2 v. 4°. London, 1849. . . . . . . 13 . 1502–3
ARCHITECTURE for general students. C. W. Horton. 16°. New York, 1874 . . . . 13 . 962
ARCTIC experiences. A history of the Polaris expedition. Ed. by E. Vale Blake. 8°. New York, 1874 . . . . 13 . 1308
ARENA (The) and the throne. L. T. Townsend. Sm. 8°. Boston, 1874 . 13 . 1175
"ARGONAUT." [*Pseud.*] *See* ROWING and training.
ARK (The) of Elm island. E. Kellogg. 16°. Boston, 1875 . . . . . 4 . 942
ARNOLD, Matthew. Higher schools and universities in Germany. Sm. 8°. London, 1874 . . . . 13 . 123
ARNOULD, *Sir* Joseph. Life of Thomas, first lord Denman, formerly lord chief justice of England. Portraits. 2 v. 8°. Boston, 1874 . 13 . 1331–32

AROUND a spring. G. Droz. 16°. New York, 1873 . . . . 4 . 861
AROUND the world in eighty days. Jules Verne. Sq. 16°. Boston, 1874. 4 . 1214
*ART of thinking. *Lord* Kames. 12°. New York, 1818 . . . . 13 . 865
ART tour to the northern capitals of Europe. J. Beavington Atkinson. 8°. New York, 1873. . . . . 13 . 144
ARTHUR Brown. E. Kellogg. 16°. Boston, 1874 . . . . 4 . 947
ARTHUR O'Leary. Charles Lever. Sm. 8°. London [n. d.] . . . . . . 4 . 401
ARTIST'S (The) love. E. D. E. N. Southworth. 12°. Philadelphia, 1872 . 4 . 1002
ARTS, manufactures, and mines, Dictionary of. Andrew Ure. 2 v. Roy. 8°. New York, 1853 . . . . 13 . 1403–4
AT home and abroad. S. M. F. Ossoli. 12°. Boston, 1874 . . . . . . 13 . 127
AT last. M. V. Terhune. 12°. New York, 1874 . . . . 4 . 1102
ATHANASIUS. *See* LIBRARY of Fathers of the Holy Catholic Church.
ATHERSTONE priory. L. N. Comyn. Sm. 8°. London [n d.] . . . . . 4 . 836
ATKINSON, J. Beavington. An art tour to northern capitals of Europe. 8°. New York, 1873 . . . . 13 . 144
ATLANTIC monthly magazine. Vols. 33 and 34. 8°. Boston, 1874 . 20 . 433–34
*ATLAS of Essex County, Mass. Roy. 4°. Philadelphia, 1872 . . . . . 15 . 1416
*Franklin County, Mass. Roy. 4°. New York, 1871 . . . . 15 . 1417
*Hampden County, Mass. Roy. 4°. New York, 1870. . . . . . . 15 . 1418
*Hampshire County, Mass. Roy. 4°. New York, 1873 . . . . . . 15 . 1419
*The State of Rhode Island and Providence Plantations. Roy. 4°. Philadelphia, 1870 . . . . 15 . 1420
*The City of Worcester, Mass. Roy. 4°. New York, 1870 . . . . 15 . 1421
*Worcester County, Mass. Roy. 4°. New York, 1870 . . . . . . 15 . 1422
AUERBACH, Berthold. Joseph in the snow. 16°. New York, 1874. . . 4 . 855
The little barefoot. Trans. by Eliza Buckminster Lee. 16°. New York, 1874 . . . . 4 . 856
Waldfried. A novel. Trans. by Simon Adler Stern. 12°. New York, 1874 . . . . 4 . 805
AUNT Jo's scrap-bag. L M. Alcott. Vol. 3. 16°. Boston, 1874 . . . 4 . 881
AUREOLA. A. S. Mackenzie. 16°. Philadelphia, 1871 . . . . 4 . 364
AURIOL. W. H. Ainsworth. 16°. London [n. d.] . . . . 4 . 1167
AUSTIN, Etta Maria, *editor*. Little people of God, and what the poets have said of them. Illustrated. 16°. Boston, 1874 . . . . 21 . 229
AUSTIN, Jane Goodwin. Moonfolk. A true account of the home of the fairy tales. Illustrated. 8°. New York, 1874 . . . . 4 . 563
AUSTRALIA. Discoveries in Central Australia, in the years 1840–41. E. J. Eyre. 2 v. 8°. London, 1845 . . . . 13 . 1216–17
AUSTRIAN government, Secret history of. Alfred Michiels. 8°. London, 1859 . . . . 13 . 1264
AUTOBIOGRAPHY. John Stuart Mill. 8°. New York, 1870 . . . . . 13 . 1245

B.

BABEL, The builders of. D. M'Causland. Sm. 8°. London, 1874 . . 13 . 1151
BABES (The) in the wood. J. De Mille. 8°. Boston, 1875 . . . . . 4 . 526
BABOLAIN. A novel. Gustave Droz. 16°. New York, 1873 . . . . . 4 . 862
BACON, Leonard. The genesis of the New England churches. With illustrations. 8° New York, 1874 . . . . 13 . 1248

BAER, *Mrs* B. F. Irene; or, beach-broken billows. 16°. New York, 1875. 4 . 461
BAILEY, James M. Life in Danbury. Illustrated. Portrait. Sq 8°. Boston, 1873 . . . . 4 . 822
BAKER, George Melville. A baker's dozen. Original humorous dialogues. 16°. Boston, 1874 . . . . 21 . 239
The drawing-room stage: a series of original dramas, comedies, farces, and entertainments for amateur theatricals and school exhibitions. 16°. Boston, 1874 . . . . 21 . 240
The exhibition drama: comprising drama, comedy, and farce, together with dramatic and musical entertainments for private theatricals, home representations, holiday and school exhibitions. Illustrated. 16°. Boston, 1875 . . . . 21 . 241
Running to waste: the story of a tomboy. Illustrated. 16°. Boston, 1875. 4 . 579
editor. Ballads of beauty. 40 full-page illustrations. Sm. 4°. Boston, 1875 . . . . 21 . 209
editor. The reading club and handy speaker. 16°. Boston, 1874 . 21 . 242
BAKER, *Sir* Samuel White. Ismailia: a narrative of the expedition to Central Africa for the suppression of the slave-trade, organized by Ismail, Khedive of Egypt. With maps, portraits, and upward of 50 full-page illustrations. L. 8°. New York, 1875 . . . . 13 . 1315
BAKER, William Munford. Mose Evans: a simple statement of the singular facts of his case. 12°. New York, 1874 . . . . 4 . 565
BAKER'S (A) dozen. Original humorous dialogues. G. M. Baker. 16°. Boston, 1874 . . . . 21 . 239
BALLADS of beauty. Ed. by G. M. Baker. Sm. 4°. Boston, 1875 . . . 21 . 209
BALLANTYNE, Robert Michael. Deep down: a tale of the Cornish mines. Illustrations. Sm. 8°. Philadelphia, 1875 . . . . 4 . 1201
The fire brigade; or, fighting the flames. Illustrated. 16°. Philadelphia [n. d.] . . . . 4 . 1202
The floating light of the Goodwin sands. Illustrated. 16°. Philadelphia [n. d.] . . . . 4 . 1203
The iron horse; or, life on the line. A tale of Grand National Trunk Railway. Illustrated. Sm. 8°. London. 1872 . . . . 4 . 1204
Man on the ocean. A book about boats and ships. Illustrated. Sm. 8°. London, 1874 . . . . 4 . 1205
The Norsemen in the west; or, America before Columbus. A tale. Illustrated. Sm. 8°. London, 1872 . . . . 4 . 1206
The pirate city. An Algerine tale. 16°. New York, 1874. 2 copies. 4 . 1207–8
Shifting winds: a story of the sea. Illustrated. 16°. Philadelphia [n. d.] 4 . 1209
The wild man of the west. A tale of the Rocky mountains. Illustrated. 16°. Philadelphia [n. d.] . . . . 4 . 1210
The young fur traders; or, snowflakes and sunbeams from the far north. Sm. 8°. Edinburgh, 1856 . . . . 4 . 1211
*BALLARD, George. Memoirs of several ladies of Great Britain, who have been celebrated for their writings, or skill in the learned languages, arts, and sciences. 4°. Oxford, 1752 . . . . 13 . 1547
*BALZAC, Honoré de. Droll stories collected from the Abbeys of Touraine. Illustrated with 425 designs by Gustave Doré Sm. 8°. London, 1874. 4 . 450
BANCROFT, George. History of the United States. Vol. 10. From 1778 to 1782. 8°. Boston, 1874 . . . . 20 . 1228

BANKER'S (The) daughter. G. W. M. Reynolds. 8°. Philadelphia [n. d.] . . . . 4 . 533
BAR (The) sinister. C. A. Collins. Sm. 8°. London [n. d.] . . . . . . 4 . 978
BARBAULD, Anna Lætitia. Life and works, by Grace Atkinson Ellis. 2 v. 12°. Boston, 1874 . . . . 13 . 167–68
BARDSLEY, Charles Wareing. Our English surnames: their sources and significations. Sm. 8°. London, 1873 . . . . 13 . 153
BARKER, Lucy D. Sale. Little wide-awake: a story book for children. With nearly 400 illustrations. Sm. 4°. London and New York, 1875. 4 . 554
BARKER, *Lady* Mary Anne. [*Mrs. Frederick Napier Broome.*] Boys. 16°. London [n. d.] . . . . 4 . 367
BARNABY Rudge. C. Dickens. 2 v. 12°. Boston, 1874 . . . . . . 4 . 1304–5
BARRINGTON. C. Lever. Sm. 8°. London [n. d.] . . . . 4 . 402
BARTHOLOMEW fair, Memoirs of. H. Morley. Sm. 8°. London [n. d.] . 13 . 1171
*BARTLETT, John Russell. The soldiers' national cemetery at Gettysburg, with the proceedings at its consecration, at the laying of the corner-stone of the monument, and its dedication. Plate, portraits, plan, and map. 4°. Providence, 1874 . . . . 13 . 1506

Note.—500 copies printed.

BARTLEY, George C. T. The schools for the people, containing the history, development, and present working of each description of English school for the industrial and poorer classes. With illustrations. 8°. London, 1871 . . . . 13 . 1418
The seven ages of a village pauper. Sm. 8°. London, 1871 . . . . 13 . 1167
BARTOL, Cyrus Augustus. The rising faith. 16°. Boston, 1874 . . . 13 . 964
BASTIAT, Frédéric. Sophisms of protection. Trans. from the Paris edition of 1863; with a preface by Horace White. 12°. New York, 1874 . . . . 13 . 942

Contents.—Part I. Sophisms of protection, first series. Part II. Sophisms of protection, second series. Part III. Spoliation and law. Part IV. Capital and interest.

BATES, Henry Walter. The naturalist on the river Amazons. A record of adventures, habits of animals, sketches of Brazilian and Indian life, and aspects of nature under the equator, during eleven years of travel. With illustrations. Sm. 8°. London, 1875 . . . . 13 . 934
BEAR and forbear. W. T. Adams. 16°. Boston, 1875 . . . . 4 . 319
BEATEN paths. Ella W. Thompson. 16°. Boston, 1874 . . . . 4 . 831
BEAUTIFUL (A) fiend. E. D. E. N. Southworth. 12°. Philadelphia, 1873. 2 copies . . . . 4 . 1003–4
BÉBÉE; or, two little wooden shoes. L. de la Rame. 12°. Philadelphia, 1874. 4 . 1141
BEC'S bedtime. S. C. Hallowell. Sm. 8°. Philadelphia, 1873 . . . . 4 . 467
BEECHER, Henry Ward. Norwood; or, village life in New England. Illustrations. 12°. New York, 1874. 2 copies . . . . 4 . 905–6
Pleasant talk about fruits, flowers, and farming. New edition with additional matter from recent writings, published and unpublished. 12°. New York, 1874 . . . . 13 . 156
Yale lectures on preaching, delivered before the theological department of Yale College, New Haven, Conn., in the regular course of the "Lyman Beecher lectureship on preaching." From phonographic reports by T. J. Ellinwood. Third series. Sm. 8°. New York, 1874. 13 . 157

BELLEW, Henry Walter. From the Indus to the Tigris. A narrative of a journey through the countries of Balochistan, Afghanistan, Khorassan and Iran, in 1872; together with a synoptical grammar and vocabulary of the Brahoe language, and a record of the meteorological observations and altitudes on the march from the Indus to the Tigris. L. 8°. London, 1874. . . . . 13 . 1329

BEN Brace. W. James. 12°. London [n. d.] . . . . 4 . 434

BEN the luggage-boy. H. Alger, jun. 16°. Boston, 1870 . . . . 4 . 1159

BENEDICT, Frank Lee. John Worthington's name. 8°. New York, 1874. 4 . 524

BENNET, William Heath. Select biographical sketches from the note-books of a law reporter. Portraits. 8°. London, 1867 . . . . 13 . 1337

BENNETT, Emerson. The outlaw's daughter; or, adventures in the south. Portrait. 12°. Philadelphia, 1874 . . . . 4 . 907

The phantom of the forest: a tale of the dark and bloody ground. 12°. Philadelphia, 1867 . . . . 4 . 908

BENSON, E. W. Boy-life, its trial, its strength, its fulness. Sundays in Wellington college, 1859–1873. A series of sermons. 8°. London, 1874. . . . . 13 . 1124

BERBER (The). W. S. Mayo. 16°. New York, 1873 . . . . 4 . 558

BESANT, Walter. The French humorists from the twelfth to the nineteenth century. 8°. Boston, 1874 . . . . 13 . 1135

BESSIE Wilmerton; or, money, and what came of it. Margaret Westcott. 12°. New York, 1874 . . . . 4 . 976

*BETHAM, William. The baronetage of England; or, the history of the English baronets, and such baronets of Scotland as are of English families; with genealogical tables, and engravings of their armorial bearings. 5v. 4°. London and Ipswich, 1801–5 . . . . 13 . 1521–25

BETROTHED (The), and The highland widow. *Sir* W. Scott. 2 v. in 1. 12°. Boston, 1874 . . . . 4 . 215

BIBLE (The) regained, and the God of the Bible ours. S. Lee. 16°. New York, 1874 . . . . 13 . 861

*BIOGRAPHIA Gallica; or, the lives of the most eminent French writers of both sexes, in divinity, philosophy, mathematics, history, poetry, &c. From the restoration of learning under Francis I. to the present time. 2 v. 12°. London, 1752. . . . . 13 . 870–71

BIOGRAPHICAL sketches. William H. Bennet. 8°. London, 1867 . . . 13 . 1337

BIRDS, Natural history of. T. R. Jones. Illustrations. Sm. 8°. London, 1874 . . . . 13 . 117

BIRDS, their cages and their keep. K. A. Buist. Sm. 8°. London, 1874 . 13 . 1144

BIVOUAC (The). W. H. Maxwell. Sm. 8°. London [n. d.] . . . . . 4 . 428

BIVOUAC and battle. W. T. Adams. 16°. Boston, 1875 . . . . 4 . 330

BLACK, William. A princess of Thule. Sm. 8°. London, 1874 . . . . 4 . 264

The strange adventures of a phaeton. Sm. 8°. London, 1874 . . . 4 . 265

BLACK (The) dwarf, and A legend of Montrose. *Sir* W. Scott. 2 v. in 1. 12°. Boston, 1873 . . . . 4 . 216

BLACKIE, John Stuart. Horæ Hellenicæ: essays and discussions on some important points of Greek philology and antiquity. 8°. London, 1874. . . . . 13 . 1064

On self-culture, intellectual, physical, and moral. 16°. New York, 1874. 13 . 866

BLACKWOOD'S magazine. Vols. 115 and 116. 8°. New York, 1874 . 18 . 1306–7

BLAKE, E. V., *editor.* Arctic experiences: containing a history of the Polaris expedition, the cruise of the Tigress, and rescue of the Polaris survivors, with a general arctic chronology. 8°. New York, 1874 . 13 . 1308
*BLANC, Charles. The grammar of painting and engraving. Trans. from the French of Blanc's "Grammaire des arts du dessin," by Kate N. Doggett. With the original illustrations. 4°. New York, 1874. . 13 . 1548
BLEAK house. C. Dickens. 2 v. 12°. Boston, 1874 . . . . 4 . 1306-7
BOAT (The) club. W. T. Adams. 16°. Boston, 1875 . . . . 4 . 308
BOGARDUS, Adam H. Field, cover, and trap shooting. Edited by Charles J. Foster. Sm. 8°. New York, 1874 . . . . 13 . 1149
BONAR, Horatius. Days and nights in the east; or, illustrations of Bible scenes. Illustrated. 16°. New York. [n. d.] . . . . 13 . 1179
*BONNEY, T. G. Lake and mountain scenery of the Swiss Alps. Illustrated with 24 photographic views, by G. Closs and O. Froeliecher. Roy. 4°. New York and Boston [n. d.] . . . . 15 . 1414
BOOK of the foundations of St. Teresa of Jesus, written by herself. Trans. from the Spanish by David Lewis. 8°. London, 1871 . . . . . 13 . 1067
*BOOK of nature, or, the history of insects. John Swammerdam, M.D. Folio, London, 1758. . . . . 15 . 1415
BOOKSELLERS. A history of booksellers. H. Curwen. Sm. 8°. London, 1873. . . . . 13 . 921
BORYS, Gontran. She loved him madly. Trans. from the original French by O. Vibeur. 12°. New York, 1874 . . . . 4 . 374
*BOSSU, Rene le. Treatise of the Epick poem: containing many curious reflexions, very useful and necessary for the right understanding and judging of the excellencies of Homer and Virgil; to which are added an essay upon Satyr, by *Mons.* D'Acier, and a treatise upon Pastoral, by *Mons.* Fontanelle. 2 v. Sm. 8°. London, 1719 . . . . . 13 . 881-82
BOSTON. Annual report of the school committee, for the year 1857. 8°. Boston, 1858. . . . . 11 . 1245
BOTHWELL: a tragedy. A. C. Swinburne. Sm. 8°. London, 1874. . . 21 . 222
BOUND to rise. H. Alger, jun. 16°. Boston, 1873 . . . . 4 . 1152
BOY (The) farmers of Elm Island. E. Kellogg. 16°. Boston, 1875 . . 4 . 943
BOY (The) hunters. M. Reid. 16°. Boston, 1874 . . . . 4 . 1238
BOY-LIFE, its trial, its strength, its fulness. E. W. Benson. 8°. London, 1874 . . . . 13 . 1124
BOY (The) slaves. M. Reid. 16°. Boston, 1874 . . . . 4 . 1239
BOY (The) tar. M. Reid. 16°. Boston, 1874 . . . . 4 . 1240
BOYESEN, Hjalmar Hjorth. Gunnar: a tale of Norse life. Sq. 16°. Boston, 1874 . . . . 4 . 888
BOYS. *Lady* M. A. Barker. 16°. London [n. d.] . . . . 4 . 367
BRACKETT, Anna C., *editor.* The education of American girls, considered in a series of essays. 12°. New York, 1874 . . . . 13 . 952
BRAKE up. W. T. Adams. 16°. Boston, 1875 . . . . 4 . 318
BRAMLEIGHS (The). C. Lever. Sm. 8°. London, 1873 . . . . 4 . 403
BRAND, John. Observations on the popular antiquities of Great Britain: chiefly illustrating the origin of our vulgar and provincial customs, ceremonies, and superstitions. Arranged, revised, and greatly enlarged by *Sir* Henry Ellis. A new edition, with further additions. 3 v. Sm. 8°. London, 1873 . . . . 13 . 106-8

*BRANDON, Raphael, and J. Arthur. An analysis of Gothick architecture: illustrated by a series of upwards of seven hundred examples of doorways, windows, &c., and accompanied with remarks on the several details of an ecclesiastical edifice. 2 v. 4°. London, 1849 . . 13 . 1502–3

BRASSY, Thomas. Life and labors of, from 1805 to 1870. *Sir* Arthur Helps. 8°. Boston, 1874 . . . . 13 . 1355

BRAVE and bold. H. Alger, jun. 16°. Boston, 1874. . . . . 4 . 1143

BRAVE (The) old salt. W. T. Adams. 16°. Boston, 1875 . . . . . . 4 . 307

BRAVO (The). J. F. Cooper. 12°. New York, 1873. . . . . 4 . 1042

BREAKING away. W. T. Adams. 16°. Boston, 1875 . . . . 4 . 322

BREATH (The). J. W. Howe. 12°. New York, 1874 . . . . 13 . 940

BRIC-A-BRAC series. *See* STODDARD, Richard Henry.

BRIDAL (The) eve. E. D. E. N. Southworth. 12°. Philadelphia, 1864 . 4 . 1006

BRIDE (The) of Lammermoor. *Sir* W. Scott. 2 v. in 1. 12°. Boston, 1873 4 . 217

BRIDE (The) of Llewellyn. E. D. E. N. Southworth. 12°. Philadelphia, 1866 4 . 1007

BRIDE'S (The) fate. E. D. E. N. Southworth 12°. Philadelphia, 1869 . 4 . 1009

BRIEF essays and brevities. G. H. Calvert. 16°. Boston, 1874 . . . . 13 . 178

BRIEF (A) history of culture. J. S. Hittell. Sm. 8°. New York, 1875 . 13 . 943

*BRIGHAM, William Tufts. Cast catalogue of antique sculpture. With an introduction to the study of ornament. 13 sheets of photographs. 4°. Boston, 1874 . . . . 13 . 1510

BROCK, *Mrs.* Carey. Home memories; or, echoes of a mother's voice. 16°. New York [n. d.] . . . . 4 . 378

BROKEN Chains. E. Warner. 8°. Boston, 1875 . . . . 4 . 523

BROOKE, Stopford A. Theology in the English poets, — Cowper, Coleridge, Wordsworth, and Burns. Sm. 8°. New York, 1875 . . . 13 . 1126

BROWNING, Robert. Sordello, a poem. 16°. London, 1840 . . . . . . 21 . 236

BRUIN. M. Reid. 16°. Boston, 1872 . . . . 4 . 1241

*BRYAN, Michael. A biographical and critical dictionary of painters and engravers, with a list of ciphers, monograms, and marks. A new edition, comprising above one thousand additional memoirs, and new plates of ciphers and monograms, by George Stanley. 4°. London, 1873 . 13 . 1526

BUCKINGHAM, Emma May. A self-made woman; or, Mary Idyl's trials and triumphs. 12°. New York, 1873 . . . . 4 . 977

BUILDING (The) of a brain. E. H. Clarke. 16°. Boston, 1874 . . . 13 . 968

BUIST, K. A. Birds, their cages and their keep; being a practical manual of bird-keeping and bird-rearing. Illustrations. Sm. 8°. London, 1874 . 13 . 1144

BULWER-LYTTON, Edward (George Earle), *Lord Lytton.* The Parisians. A novel. Illustrated. 2 v. in 1. 12°. New York, 1874 . . . . 4 . 481

Another edition. 3 v. in 1. 16°. Philadelphia, 1874 . . . . 4 . 482

BULWER-LYTTON (Edward) Robert, *Lord Lytton.* Fables in song. 16°. Boston, 1874 . . . . 21 . 250

BURRITT, Elihu. Ten-minute talks on all sorts of topics. With an autobiography of the author. 16°. Boston, 1874 . . . . 13 . 959

BURTON, Richard Francis. A mission to Gelele king of Dahome. With notices of the so-called "Amazons," the grand customs, the human sacrifices, the present state of the slave-trade, and the Negro's place in nature. 2 plates. 2 v. Sm. 8°. London, 1864 . . . . 13 . 141–42

BURY, *Baroness* Blaze de. Germania, its courts, camps, and people. 2 v. 8°. London, 1850 . . . . 13 . 1322–23

Bush-boys (The). M. Reid. 16°. Boston, 1874 . . . . 4 . 1242
Bushrangers (The). W. H. Thomes. 12°. Boston, 1875 . . . . . . 4 . 1132
Busk, *Miss* R. H. The valleys of Tirol, their traditions and customs, and how to visit them. 1 plate, and maps. Sm. 8°. London, 1874 . . 13 . 936
Butler, William Archer. Lectures on the history of ancient philosophy. Edited from the author's MSS., with notes by William Hepworth Thompson. 8°. London, 1874 . . . . 13 . 1419
Butler, W. F. The wild north land; being the story of a winter journey, with dogs, across northern North America. With illustrations and route map. Portrait. 8°. London, 1874 . . . . 13 . 1156
By still waters. Isabella F. Mayo. Sm. 8°. New York, 1874 . . . . 4 . 269

C.

Cairnes, J. E. Some leading principles of political economy newly expounded. 8°. New York, 1874 . . . . 13 . 1341
Caleb Krinkle. C. C. Coffin. Sm. 8°. Boston, 1875 . . . . 4 . 256
Calverley, C. S. Fly-leaves. 16°. New York, 1872 . . . . 21 . 249
Calvert, George H. Brief essays and brevities. 16°. Boston, 1874 . . 13 . 178
*Camerario, Joachimo. Symbolorum et emblematum ex re herbaria desumtorum centuria una. 4°. Norimberg, 1590 . . . . 13 . 914
Cameron (The) Pride. M. J. Holmes. 12°. New York, 1874. 2 copies. 3 . 1335–36
Campaigning on the Oxus, and the fall of Khiva. J. A. MacGahan. 8°. New York, 1874 . . . . 13 . 1353
Campbell, L. J., and Root, O., jun., *editors*. The Columbian speaker. 16°. Boston, 1874 . . . . 4 . 851
Canada. The old régime in Canada. 1653 to 1763. Francis Parkman. 8°. Boston, 1874 . . . . 13 . 1138
Capes, J. M. The mosaic-worker's daughter. A novel. 3 v. Sm. 8°. London, 1868 . . . . 4 . 801–3
"Carleton" [*Pseud.*]. *See* Coffin, Charles Carleton.
Carlyle, Thomas. The life of John Sterling. 16°. New York, 1871 . 13 . 867
*Caroline of Brunswick. G. W. M. Reynolds. 8°. Philadelphia [n. d.] 4 . 541
Caroll, Martha. How Marjory helped. Illustrated. 16°. Boston, 1874. 4 . 567
Carpenter, William Benjamin. Principles of human physiology, with their chief applications to pathology, hygiene, and forensic medicine. Third American, from the last London edition. With notes and additions by Meredith Clymer. 317 wood-cut and other illustrations. 8°. Philadelphia, 1847 . . . . 13 . 1425
— Principles of mental physiology, with their applications to the training and discipline of the mind and the study of its morbid conditions. 8°. New York, 1874 . . . . 13 . 1265
Cary, Alice. Clovernook children. 16°. Boston, 1855 . . . . 4 . 823
Castelar, Emilio. Old Rome and New Italy. (Recuerdos de Italia.) Trans. by *Mrs.* Arthur Arnold. Sm. 8°. New York, 1874 . . . 13 . 1270
Castlemon, Harry [*Pseud.*]. *See* Fosdick, Charles A.
Castleton, D. R. Salem. A tale of the 17th century. 16°. N.Y., 1874. 4 . 267

Note.— The events connected with the witchcraft delusion at Salem have been made the basis of many tales. For the historical authorities on the subject, see Salem witchcraft, by C. W. Upham, 2 v. (17.241–2), and by R. Calef (14.171).

CATACOMBS (The) of Rome. W. H. Withrow. Sm. 8°. New York, 1874. 13 . 1141
*CATALOGUES. Andover, Mass. Catalogue of the Memorial hall library. Sq. 8°. Lawrence, 1874 . . . . 12 . 501
*Baltimore, Md. Catalogue of the English prose fiction, including translations and juvenile fiction, in the Mercantile library association of Baltimore, to October, 1874. 8°. Baltimore, 1874 . . . . 12 . 502
*Boston public library. A catalogue of books belonging to the Lower Hall of the central department, in the classes of history, biography, and travel. 8°. Boston, 1873 . . . . 12 . 503
*Lower Hall. Books of English prose fiction, including translations, juvenile fiction, and some juvenile works not fiction. 8°. Boston, 1871 . . . . 12 , 504
*Lower Hall. Poetry, drama, collections, periodicals, and miscellaneous works. 8°. Boston, 1870 . . . . 12 . 505
*Lower Hall. Works in the arts and sciences. 8°. Boston, 1871 . 12 . 506
*Brighton, Mass. Second catalogue of the Holton library of Brighton. 8°. Boston, 1872 . . . . 12 . 507
*Brookline, Mass. Catalogue of the public library of Brookline. 8°. Cambridge, 1873 . . . . 12 . 508
*Northampton. Catalogue of the public library of Northampton. 8°. Northampton, 1874 . . . . 12 . 509
*Winchester. By-laws and catalogue of the town library, Winchester, Mass. 8°. Woburn, 1874 . . . . 12 . 510
CATS: their points and characteristics. G. W. Stables. Sm. 8°. London [n. d.] . . . . 13 . 176
CAXTON, Laura [*Pseud.*]. *See* COMINS, Lizzie B.
CELEBRITIES of the past and present. M. Maceuen. Sm. 8°. Philadelphia, 1874 . . . . 13 . 1268
CHAFFERS, William. The collector's hand-book of marks and monograms on pottery and porcelain of the renaissance and modern periods, selected from his larger work entitled "Marks and monograms on pottery and porcelain." Fourth edition, 1874, with nearly 3,000 marks. Sm. 8°. London, 1874 . . . . 13 . 856
CHAINBEARER (The). J. F. Cooper. 12°. New York. 1873 . . . . 4 . 1043
CHALLICE, A. E. Memories of French palaces. Illustrated. 8°. London, 1871 . . . . 13 . 1148
CHAMIER, Captain [*Pseud.*]. *See* JAMES, William.
CHANEY, George L. F. Grant & Co.; or, partnerships. A story for boys who "mean business." 16°. Boston, 1875 . . . . 4 . 379
CHANGED (The) brides. E. D. E. N. Southworth. 12°. Philadelphia, 1869. 4 . 1008
CHANNING, William Ellery. Conversations in Rome. 16°. Boston, 1847. 13 . 828
Memoir of, with extracts from his correspondence and MSS. 3 v. 12°. Boston, 1848. . . . . 13 . 829–31
Works. 8th ed. 6 v. 12°. Boston, 1848 . . . . 13 . 832–37

Vol. I. Character and writings of John Milton; Character of Napoleon Bonaparte; Character and writings of Fénélon; Moral argument against Calvinism: National literature; Remarks on associations; The Union; Remarks on education.
II. Slavery; Abolitionists; Annexation of Texas; Catholicism; Creeds; Temperance; Self-Culture.
III. Preaching Christ; War; Unitarian Christianity; The evidences of revealed religion; The demands of the age on the minis-

CHANNING, William E. Works. Vol. III. (*continued*).

try; Unitarian Christianity most favorable to piety; The great purpose of Christianity; Likeness to God; The Christian ministry; Duties of children; Honor due to all men; Evidences of Christianity.
IV. Character of Christ; Christianity a rational religion: Spiritual freedom; Self-denial; Imitableness of Christ's character; Evil of sin; Immortality; Love to Christ; The future life; War; Ministry for the poor; Christian worship; The Sunday school; The philanthropist.
V. The slavery question; Lecture on war; Lectures on the elevation of the laboring portion of the community; Discourse on the death of the *Rev* Dr. Follen; Charges at the ordinations of C. Barnard, F. T. Gray, R. C. Waterston, and J. S. Dwight; Miscellanies: Appendix
VI. Emancipations; Life and character of the *Rev.* Joseph Tuckerman, D.D; The present ages; The Church; Duty of the free states; Address on the anniversary of emancipation in the West Indies.

CHANNING, W. E., and AIKIN, Lucy. Correspondence, from 1826 to 1842. Edited by A. L. LeBreton. Sm. 8°. London, 1874 . . . . 13 . 838

CHAPMAN, George. Works. Plays, edited, with notes, by Richard Herne Shepherd. Portrait. Sm. 8°. London, 1874 . . . . 21 . 227

Contents.—The blind beggar of Alexandria; An humorous day's mirth; All fools; The gentleman usher; Monsieur d'Olive; Bussy d'Ambois; The revenge of Bussy d'Ambois; Byron's conspiracy; The tragedy of Charles, duke of Byron; May-day; The widow's tears; The mask of the Middle temple and Lincoln's inn; The tragedy of Cæsar and Pompey; Alphonus emperor of Germany; Revenge for honor. Plays written in conjunction with Ben Jonson. Marston, and Shirley: Eastward ho; The ball; The tragedy of Philip Chabot, admiral of France.

CHARLES I. Historical notices of events in the reign of Charles I. N. Wallington. 2 v. Sm. 8°. London, 1869 . . . . 13 . 148–49

CHARLES O'Malley. C. Lever. Sm. 8°. London, 1872 . . . . . . 4 . 404

CHARLEY Laurel. W. H. G. Kingston. Sm. 8°. London [n. d.] 2 copies . . . . 4 . 929–30

CHARLIE Bell of Elm island. E. Kellogg. 16°. Boston, 1875 . . . . 4 . 941

CHARLIE Codman's cruise. H. Alger, jun. 16°. Boston, 1866 . . . . 4 . 1146

CHARMING (A) widow. K. S. Macquoid. 12°. New York, 1874 . . . 4 . 366

CHASE, Henry, and SANBORN, Charles W. The north and the south: a statistical view of the condition of the free and slave States. Compiled from official documents. 12°. Boston, 1856 . . . . 13 . 855

CHASTE as ice and pure as snow. *Mrs.* M. C. Despard. Sm. 8°. Philadelphia [n. d.] . . . . 4 . 560

CHATTERTON: a story of the year 1770. D. Masson. Sm. 8°. London, 1874 . . . . 13 . 104

CHEMICAL analysis, Commercial hand-book of. A. Normandy. 12°. London, 1850 . . . . 13 . 849

CHEMICAL analysis, Instructions in, quantitative. C. R. Fresenius. 8°. London, 1846 . . . . 13 . 1406

CHEMICAL analysis, qualitative and quantitative. Henry M. Noad. 8°. Philadelphia, 1849 . . . . 13 . 1208

CHEMICAL and geological essays. T. S. Hunt. 8°. Boston, 1875 . . . 13 . 1132

CHEMICAL and pharmaceutic manipulations. Campbell Morfit. 8°. Philadelphia, 1849 . . . . 13 . 1209

CHEMICALS, drugs, medicines, &c., Examinations of. C. H. Peirce. 12°. Philadelphia, 1853 . . . . 13 . 848

CHEMISTRY in its applications to agriculture and physiology. Justus Liebig. 12°. New York, 1847 . . . . 13 . 847
CHEMISTRY. The new chemistry. Josiah P. Cooke, jun. 12°. New York, 1874 . . . . 13 . 1154
CHEMISTRY, organic and physiological, Principles of. *Dr.* Carl Löwig. 8°. Philadelphia, 1853 . . . . 13 . 1405
CHENEY, Ednah D. The child of the tide. 16°. Boston, 1875 . . . . 4 . 370
CHERBULIEZ, Victor. Count Kostia. Trans from the French by O. D. Ashley. 16°. New York, 1873 . . . . 4 . 857
Joseph Noirel's revenge. Trans. from the French by William F. West. 16°. New York, 1872 . . . . 4 . 858
Prosper. Trans. from the French by Carl Benson. 16°. New York, 1874 . . . . 4 . 859
CHILD, Francis James, *editor.* English and Scottish ballads. 8 v. Sm. 8°. Boston, 1860 . . . . 21 . 214–21
CHILD (The) of the island glen. E. Kellogg. 16°. Boston, 1874 . . . 4 . 950
CHILD (The) of the tide. E. D. Cheney. 16°. Boston, 1875 . . . . 4 . 370
CHILD world. M. A. Dodge. 2 v. Sq. 16°. Boston, 1873 . . . . . 4 . 580–81
CHILDHOOD songs. Lucy Larcom. Sq. 8°. Boston, 1875 . . . . 21 . 226
CHILD'S (A) history of England. C. Dickens. 12°. Boston, 1871 . . . 4 . 1308
CHORLEY, Henry F. Recent art and society, as described in (his) autobiography and memoirs. Compiled from the edition of Henry G. Hewlett, by C. H. Jones. Sm. 8°. New York, 1874. . . . . . . 13 . 1267
CHRIST, The Life of. Frederic W. Farrar. 2 v. 8°. New York, 1874. 13 . 1342–43
CHRISTIAN (The) in the world. D. W. Faunce. 16°. Boston, 1875 . . 13 . 1174
CHRISTIAN theology for the people. W. Lord. 8°. New York, 1875 . . 13 . 1316
CHRISTLIEB, Theodore. Modern doubt and Christian belief. A series of apologetic lectures addressed to earnest seekers after truth. Trans. with the author's sanction, chiefly by H. U. Weitbrecht, and edited by T. L. Kingsbury. 8°. New York, 1874 . . . . 13 . 1317
CHRISTIANITY and science. A. P. Peabody. Sm. 8°. New York, 1874 . 13 . 937
CHRISTIANITY the science of manhood. M. J. Savage. 16°. Boston, 1875 . . . . 13 . 1147
CHRISTIANITY, The secret of. S. S. Hebbard. 16°. Boston, 1874 . . . 13 . 154
CHRISTMAS books. C. Dickens. 12°. Boston, 1871 . . . . 4 . 1309
CHRISTMAS (The) guest. E. D. E. N. Southworth, and F. H. Baden. 12°. Philadelphia, 1870 . . . . 4 . 1039
CHRISTOPHER Crooked. W. E. Hathaway. 16°. New York, 1873 . . . 4 . 843
*CHRONOLOGY and geography, history and prophecy, A new analysis of. W. Hales. 4 v. 8°. London, 1830 . . . . 13 . 1554–57
CHURCH, R. W. The sacred poetry of early religions. Two lectures delivered in St. Paul's Cathedral, Jan. 27 and Feb. 3, 1874. Sm. 8°. London, 1874 . . . . 21 . 252
CHURCH (The) and the Empires. H. W. Wilberforce. 8°. London, 1874 . 13 . 1240
CHURCH of our fathers. Daniel Rock. 4 v. 8°. London, 1849 . . 13 . 1056–59
CIRCUIT (The) rider. E. Eggleston. 12°. New York, 1874 . . . . . 4 . 456
CLARE Savile; or, sixty years ago. Julia Luard. Sm. 8°. London. [n. d.] . . . . 4 . 806
CLARKE, Edward H. The building of a brain. 16°. Boston, 1874 . . . 13 . 968
Sex in education; or, a fair chance for the girls. 16°. Boston, 1874 . 13 . 862

CLARKE, Mary Cowden. The girlhood of Shakspeare's heroines; in a series of tales. Sq. 8°. New York, 1873 . . . . 4 . 804
The trust and the remittance. 16°. Boston, 1874 . . . . 21 . 238
CLARKE, R. S. [*Sophie May.*] Our Helen. Illustrated. 16°. Boston, 1875 4 . 840
CLEMENS, Samuel L. [*Mark Twain*], and WARNER, Charles Dudley. The gilded age; a tale of to-day. With illustrations. 8°. Hartford, 1874. 4 . 546
CLEMENT, Clara Erskine. Painters, sculptors, architects, engravers, and their works. With illustrations and monograms. Sm. 8°. New York, 1874 . . . . 13 . 146
CLEVELAND, Cecilia. The story of a summer (at Horace Greeley's home); or, journal leaves from Chappaqua. Sq. 16°. New York, 1874 . . 4 . 883
CLIFF-CLIMBERS (The). M. Reid. 16°. Boston. 1874 . . . . 4 . 1254
CLIQUE (The) of gold. E. Gaboriau. 8°. Boston, 1874 . . . . 4 . 527
CLOISTER (The) and the hearth. C. Reade. Sm. 8°. Boston, 1872 . . 4 . 1118
CLOVERNOOK children. Alice Cary. 16°. Boston, 1855 . . . . 4 . 823
COBDEN, Paul [*Pseud.*]. Take a peep. 16°. Boston, 1874 . . . . . . 4 . 438
COCKTON, Henry. The love match. Sm. 8°. London [n. d.] . . . . 4 . 577
COFFIN, Charles Carleton. [*Carleton.*] Caleb Krinkle: a story of American life. Sm. 8°. Boston, 1875 . . . . 4 . 256
Following the flag, from August, 1861, to November, 1862, with the army of the Potomac. Illustrated. 16°. Boston, 1865 . . . . 4 . 257
COLERIDGE, *Sir* J. T. Memoir of the Rev. John Keble, M. A. Sm. 8°. London, 1874 . . . . 13 . 158
COLERIDGE, Samuel T. Confessions of an inquiring spirit. 16°. Boston, 1841 . . . . 13 . 860
COLERIDGE, Sara. Memoirs and letters. Edited by her daughter. 8°. New York, 1874 . . . . 13 . 1236
Phantasmion. A fairy tale. 12°. Boston, 1874 . . . . 4 . 1073
COLLINS, Charles Allston. The bar sinister. A tale. Sm. 8°. London [n. d.] . . . . 4 . 978
COLLINS (William) Wilkie. The dead alive. Illustrated. 16°. Boston, 1874 . . . . 4 . 358
The frozen deep. Illustrated. 12°. Boston, 1875. 3 copies . 4 . 359-60-61
My miscellanies. Portrait. 12°. New York, 1874 . . . . 4 . 362
COLLYER, Robert. A man in earnest; life of A. H. Conant. 16°. Boston, 1875 . . . . 13 . 864
COLMAN, James F. The knightly heart, and other poems. 16°. Boston, 1873 . . . . 21 . 230
COLUMBIAN (The) speaker. Edited by L. J. Campbell, and O. Root, jun. 16°. Boston, 1874 . . . . 4 . 851
COMBE, Andrew. Treatise on the physiological and moral management of infancy. With notes and a supplementary chapter by John Bell, M. D. 12°. Philadelphia, 1842 . . . . 13 . 850
COMING (The) wave. W. T. Adams. 16°. Boston, 1875 . . . . . . 4 . 341
COMINS, Lizzie B. [*Laura Caxton.*] Marion Berkley: a story for girls. Illustrated. 16°. Boston, 1870 . . . . 4 . 464
COMPARATIVE (A) history of religions. J. C. Moffat. Part 2. 16°. New York, 1873 . . . . 13 . 173
COMYN, L. N. Atherstone priory. Sm. 8°. London [n. d.] . . . . . 4 . 836
CON Cregan. C. Lever. Sm. 8°. London [n.d.] . . . . 4 . 405

CONANT, Augustus Hammond, Life of. R. Collyer. 16°. Boston, 1875 . 13 . 864
CONFESSIONS of an inquiring spirit. S. T. Coleridge. 16°. Boston, 1841. 13 . 860
CONQUEST of the sea. H. Siebe. Sm. 8°. London, 1873 . . . . 13 . 967
CONSERVATION (The) of energy. B. Stewart. Sm. 8°. New York, 1874. 13 . 136
CONWAY, Moncure Daniel. The earthward pilgrimage. 16°. New York, 1874 . . . . 13 . 160
Editor. The sacred anthology. A book of ethnical scriptures. 8°. New York, 1874 . . . . 13 . 1068
COOKE, John Esten. Justin Harley: a romance of old Virginia. Illustrated. 12°. Philadelphia, 1874 . . . . 4 . 458
Pretty Mrs. Gaston, and other stories. Illustrated. 16°. New York, 1874 . . . . 4 . 457
COOKE, Josiah Parsons, jun. The new chemistry. 12°. New York, 1874. 13 . 1154
COOLIDGE, Susan [*Pseud.*]. *See* WOOLSEY, S. C.
COOMASSIE and Magdala: the story of two British campaigns in Africa. H. M. Stanley. 8°. New York, 1874 . . . . .13 . 1309
COOPER, James Fenimore. Afloat and ashore. A sea tale. 12°. New York, 1873 . . . . 4 . 1040
Miles Wallingford. *A sequel* to Afloat and ashore. 12°. New York, 1873 . . . . 4 . 1041
The bravo. 12°. New York, 1873 . . . . 4 . 1042
The Chainbearer; or, the Littlepage manuscripts. 12°. New York, 1873 . . . . 4 . 1043
The Redskins; or, Indian and Injin: being the conclusion of the Littlepage manuscripts. 12°. New York, 1873 . . . . 4 . 1044
The crater; or, Vulcan's peak. A tale of the Pacific. 12°. New York, 1873 . . . . 4 . 1045
The deerslayer; or, the first war-path. 12°. New York, 1873 . . . 4 . 1046
The headsman; or, the Abbaye des Vignerons. 12°. New York, 1873. 4 . 1047
The Heidenmauer; or, the Benedictines. A legend of the Rhine. 12°. New York, 1873 . . . . 4 . 1048
Homeward Bound; or, the chase. A tale of the sea. 12°. New York, 1873 . . . . 4 . 1049
Home as found. *A sequel* to Homeward bound. 12°. New York, 1873 4. 1 050
Jack Tier; or, the Florida reef. 12°. New York, 1873 . . . . . . 4 . 1051
The last of the Mohicans. A tale of 1757. 12°. New York, 1875 . 4 . 1052
Lionel Lincoln; or, the leaguer of Boston. 12°. New York, 1873 . 4 . 1053
Mercedes of Castile; or, the voyage to Cathay. 12°. New York, 1873 4 . 1054
The Monikins. 12°. New York, 1873 . . . . 4 . 1055
Oak-openings; or, the bee-hunter. 12°. New York, 1873 . . . . 4 . 1056
The pathfinder; or, the inland sea. 12°. New York, 1874 . . . . 4 . 1057
The pilot. A tale of the sea. 12°. New York, 1872 . . . . 4 . 1058
The pioneers; or, the sources of the Susquehanna. 12°. New York, 1875 . . . . 4 . 1059
The prairie. 12°. New York, 1873 . . . . 4 . 1060
Precaution. 12°. New York, 1873 . . . . 4 . 1061
The red rover. 12°. New York, 1872 . . . . 4 . 1062
Satanstoe. 12°. New York, 1873 . . . . 4 . 1063
The sea-lions; or, the lost sealers. 12°. New York, 1873 . . . . 4 . 1064
The spy. A tale of the neutral ground. 12°. New York, 1874 . . 4 . 1065

COOPER, James Fenimore (*continued*).
The two admirals. 12°. New York, 1873 . . . . 4 . 1066
The Water-witch; or, the skimmer of the seas. 12°. New York, 1873 . 4 . 1067
The ways of the hour. 12°. New York, 1873 . . . . 4 . 1068
The Wept of Wish-Ton-Wish. 12°. New York, 1873 . . . . 4 . 1069
The Wing-and-wing; or, Le Feu-follet. 12°. New York, 1873 . . . 4 . 1070
Wyandotté; or, the hutted knoll. 12°. New York, 1873 . . . . . . 4 . 1071

Note.—Five of the above form the "Leatherstocking tales," in the following order: The deerslayer, Last of the Mohicans, The pathfinder, The pioneers, and The prairie.

COOPER, Thomas. Old-fashioned stories. Sm. 8°. London, 1874 . . . 4 . 463
CORRESPONDENCE of William Ellery Channing, D.D., and Lucy Aikin, from 1826 to 1842. Ed. by A. L. Le Breton. Sm. 8°. Boston, 1874 . . . . 13 . 838
COULANGE, Numa Denis Fustel de. *See* FUSTEL DE COULANGES, Numa Denis.
COUNT Christoval. G. W. M. Reynolds. 8°. Philadelphia [n. d.) . . . 4 . 536
COUNT Kostia. V. Cherbuliez. 16°. New York, 1873 . . . . 4 . 857
COUNT Robert of Paris. *Sir* W. Scott. 2 v. in 1. 12°. Boston, 1869. . 4 . 218
COUSIN Geoffry. T. Hook. 16°. London [n. d.] . . . . 4 . 808
COUSIN Maude and Rosamond. M. J. Holmes. 12°. New York, 1874. 2 copies . . . . 3 . 1337–38
COUSIN William. T. Hook. 16°. London [n. d.] . . . . 4 . 809
COWLES, *Rev.* Henry. Hebrew history, from the death of Moses to the close of the Scripture narrative. 21°. New York, 1875 . . . . . . 13 . 1263
COX, George W. The crusades. With a map. 16°. New York, 1874 . 13 . 873
CRAIK, Dinah Maria, *formerly Miss Mulock.* The little lame prince and his travelling-cloak. Illustrated. Sq. 16°. New York, 1875 . . . . 4 . 454
My mother and I. A love story. Sm. 8°. New York, 1874 . . . 4 . 455
CRAIK, Georgiana M. Miss Moore: a tale for girls. 16°. New York, 1874 . . . . 4 . 874
CRATER (The). J. F. Cooper. 12°. New York, 1873 . . . . 4 . 1045
CRAVEN, *Mme.* A. Fleurange. Trans. from the French by M. M. R. 16°. New York, 1873 . . . . 4 . 860
CRETAN (The) insurrection of 1866–68. W. J. Stillman. 8°. New York, 1874 . . . . 13 . 137
CRICHTON. W. H. Ainsworth. 16°. London [n. d.] . . . . 4 . 1168
CRINGLE and cross-tree. W. T. Adams. 16°. Boston, 1875 . . . . . . 4 . 329
CROLY, Jennie Cunningham. [*Jennie June.*] For better or worse: a book for some men, and all women. 16°. Boston, 1875 . . . . 4 . 373
CROSS and Crescent. W. T. Adams. 16°. Boston, 1874 . . . . 4 . 351
CROSS (The) of Berney; or, Irene's lovers. *Mme.* E. de Girardin; Théophile Gautier; Jules Sandeau; Jules Mery. 12°. Philadelphia, 1873. 2 copies . . . . 4 . 911–12
CROWNED in palm-land. M. C. Nassau. 12°. Philadelphia, 1874 . . . 13 . 1157
CRUEL as the grave. E. D. E. N. Southworth. 12°. Philadelphia, 1871 . 4 . 1010
CRUISE (The) of the Casco. E. Kellogg. 16°. Boston, 1874 . . . . . 4 . 949
CRUSADES (The). George W. Cox. 16°. New York, 1874 . . . . . . 13 . 873
CUDLIP, Annie. [*Annie Thomas.*] No alternative. A novel. Sm. 8°. Philadelphia [n. d.]. 2 copies . . . . 4 . 917–18

CURSE (The) of Clifton. E. D. E. N. Southworth. 12°. Philadelphia, 1874 . . . . 4 . 1012

CURTIUS, Ernst. The history of Greece. Trans. by Adolphus William Ward. 5 v. 12°. New York, 1874 . . . . 13 . 1127–31

CURWEN, Henry. A history of booksellers, the old and the new. With portraits and illustrations. Sm. 8°. London, 1873 . . . . 13 . 921

CUSTER, *Gen.* G. A. My life on the plains; or, personal exp'riences with Indians. Illustrated. 8°. New York, 1874 . . . . 13 . 1069

D.

DALTON, William. Will Adams, the first Englishman in Japan. A romantic biography. Illustrated. Sm. 8°. London [n. d.] . . . . . . 4 . 571

DALTONS, (The). C. Lever. Sm. 8°. London, 1872 . . . . 4 . 406

DANGEROUS (A) Game. Edmund Yates. 8°. Boston, 1874 . . . . . . 4 . 530

DARKNESS and daylight. M. J. Holmes. 12°. New York, 1874. 2 copies. 3 . 1339–40

DAVENPORT Dunn. C. Lever. Sm. 8°. London, 1872 . . . . 4 . 407

DAVID Copperfield. C. Dickens. 2 v. 12°. Boston, 1872 . . . 4 . 1310–11

DAVID, King of Israel. W. M. Taylor. 8°. New York, 1875 . . . . 13 . 1125

DAVID Lloyd's last will. H. Smith. 16°. New York [n. d.] . . . . . . 4 . 876

DAVIES, Theodore. Losing to win. A novel. 12°. New York, 1874 . . 4 . 266

DAVIS, William M. Nimrod of the sea; or, the American whaler. Illustrated. 12°. New York, 1874 . . . . 4 . 363

DAY'S (A) ride. C. Lever. Sm. 8°. London [n. d.] . . . . 4 . 408

DAYS and nights in the east. H. Bonar. 16°. New York [n. d.] . . . 13 . 1179

DEACONS. W. H. H. Murray. Sq. 16°. Boston, 1875 . . . . 4 . 555

DEAD (The) alive. W. Collins. 16°. Boston, 1874 . . . . 4 . 358

DEEP down: a tale of the Cornish mines. R. M. Ballantyne. Sm. 8°. Philadelphia, 1875 . . . . 4 . 1201

DEERSLAYER (The). J. F. Cooper. 12°. New York, 1873 . . . . . . 4 . 1046

DE FOREST, J. W. Honest John Vane. 16°. New Haven, 1875 . . . 4 . 936

DE MILLE, James. The babes in the wood. 8°. Boston, 1875 . . . . 4 . 526

The lily and the cross. A tale of Acadia. Illustrated. 12°. Boston, 1875. 2 copies . . . . 4 . 913–14

DEMOCRACY and monarchy in France. C. K. Adams. 8°. N.Y., 1874. 13 . 1356

DENHAM, Dixon, and CLAPPERTON, Hugh. Narrative of travels and discoveries in Northern and Central Africa, in the years 1822, 1823, and 1824. 2 v. 8°. London, 1824 . . . . 13 . 1232–33

Note.—This work is a narrative of the travels of Major Denham, Capt. Clapperton, and Dr. Oudney, across the great desert to the tenth degree of northern latitude; and from Kouka in Bornou, to Sackatoo, the capital of the Felatah empire.

DENSEL, Mary. Lloyd Dalan. (Juvenile.) Illustrated. 16°. N.Y., 1874. 4 . 879

DESERT (The) home. M. Reid. 16°. Boston, 1872 . . . . 4 . 1243

DESERTED (The) ship. C. Howe. Sm. 8°. London, 1873 . . . . . . 4 . 875

DESERTED (The) wife. E. D. E. N. Southworth. 12°. Phila. (1855) . . 4 . 1013

DESK and debit. W. T. Adams. 16°. Boston, 1875 . . . . 4 . 328

DESPARD, *Mrs.* M. C. Chaste as ice and pure as snow. A novel. Sm. 8°. Philadelphia [n. d.] . . . . 4 . 560

DESPERATE remedies. Thomas Hardy. 16°. New York, 1874 . . . . 4 . 864
DESTINY. M. Ferrier. 16°. London [n. d.] . . . . 4 . 824
DETLEF, Carl. Valentine, the countess; or, between father and son. Trans. from the German by M. S. 12°. Philadelphia, 1874 . . . . . . 4 . 259
DEUTSCH, Emanuel Oscar Menahem, Literary remains of. With a brief memoir. 8°. New York, 1874 . . . . 13 . 1230
DE VERE, Aubrey. Legends of Saint Patrick. Sm. 8°. London, 1872 . 21 . 237
DIAMOND cut diamond. T. Adolphus Trollope. 16°. New York, 1874. 4 . 466
DIAZ, Abby Morton. Lucy Maria. Illustrated. 16°. Boston, 1874 . . 4 . 935
DICKENS, Charles (John Huffam). Barnaby Rudge. Illustrated. 2 v. 12°. Boston, 1874 . . . . 4 . 1304–5
Bleak house. Illustrated. 2 v. 12°. Boston, 1874 . . . . . . 4 . 1306–7
Child's (A) history of England, also a Holiday romance, and other pieces. Illustrated. 12°. Boston, 1871 . . . . 4 . 1308
Christmas books. Illustrated. 12°. Boston, 1871 . . . . 4 . 1309
David Copperfield. Illustrated. 2 v. 12°. Boston, 1872 . . . 4 . 1310–11
Dombey and son. Illustrated. 2 v. 12°. Boston, 1875 . . . . 4 . 1312–13
Great expectations. Illustrated. 12°. Boston, 1874 . . . . 4 . 1314
Little Dorrit. Illustrated. 2 v. 12°. Boston, 1875 . . . . . . 4 . 1315–16
Martin Chuzzlewit. Illustrated. 2. v. 12°. Boston, 1872 . . . 4 . 1317–18
Mystery (The) of Edwin Drood, and other stories. Illustrated. 12°. Boston, 1871 . . . . 4 . 1319
Nicholas Nickleby. Illustrated. 2 v. 12°. Boston, 1871 . . . 4 . 1320–21
Old (The) curiosity shop. Illustrated. 2 v. 12°. Boston, 1874. 4 . 1322–23
Oliver Twist. Illustrated. 12°. Boston, 1871 . . . . 4 . 1324
Our mutual friend. Illustrated. 2 v. 12°. Boston, 1874 . . . 4 . 1325–26
Pickwick papers. Illustrated. 2 v. 12°. Boston, 1875 . . . . 4 . 1327–28
Pictures from Italy, and American notes. Illustrated. 12°. Boston, 1871 . . . . 4 . 1329
Sketches by Boz. Illustrated. 12°. Boston [n. d.] . . . . 4 . 1330
Tale (A) of two cities. Illustrated. 12°. Boston, 1874 . . . . . . 4 . 1331
Uncommercial traveller, and additional Christmas stories. Illustrated. 12°. Boston, 1872 . . . . 4 . 1332
DICKENS, Charles, Life of. J. Forster. Vol. 3. 12°. Philadelphia, 1874. 13 . 162
DICKENS, Charles. Schools and schoolmasters. Ed. by J. T. Chapman. 12°. New York, 1871 . . . . 4 . 1333
DICTIONARY of arts, manufactures, and mines. Illustrated. Andrew Ure. 2 v. Roy. 8°. New York, 1853 . . . . 13 . 1403–4
*DICTIONARY of the English language. C. Richardson. 2 v. 4°. London, 1867. Vol. 1, A–K: Vol. 2, L–Z . . . . 13 . 1511–12
*DICTIONARY of painters and engravers. Michael Bryan. 4°. London, 1873 . . . . 13 . 1526
DIKES and ditches. W. T. Adams. 16°. Boston, 1875 . . . . 4 . 346
DISCARDED (The) daughter. E. D. E. N. Southworth. 12°. Phila., 1852. 4 . 1014
DODD (The) family abroad. C. Lever. Sm. 8°. London, 1872 . . . . 4 . 409
DODGE, Mary Abigail. [*Gail Hamilton.*] Child-world. (Juvenile.) Illustrated. 2 v. Sq. 16°. Boston, 1873 . . . . 4 . 580–81
Nursery noonings. 16°. New York, 1875 . . . . 4 . 582
Twelve miles from a lemon. [Essays.] 16°. New York, 1874 . . . 4 . 583
DODGE, Mary Mapes. Rhymes and jingles. Illustrated. 16°. N.Y., 1875. 21 . 228

DOG (The) fiend; or, Snarleyyow. F. Marryat. 12°. London, 1873 . . 4 . 237
DOMBEY and son. C. Dickens. 2 v. 12°. Boston 1875 . . . . . . 4 . 1312–13
DONALDSON, James. The apostolical fathers: a critical account of their genuine writings and of their doctrines. Sm. 8°. London, 1874 . 13 . 155
DOORS outward. S. C. Robbins. 16°. New York, 1875 . . . . 4 . 850
DORA Deane, and Maggie Miller. M. J. Holmes. 12°. New York, 1874. 2 copies . . . . 3 . 1341–42
DORCAS (The) club. W. T. Adams. 16°. Boston, 1875 . . . . 4 . 342
DOUGLAS, Amanda M. The old woman who lived in a shoe. Illustrated. 16°. Boston, 1875 . . . . 4 . 572
DOWN the Rhine. W. T. Adams. 16°. Boston, 1875 . . . . 4 . 348
DOWN the river. W. T. Adams. 16°. Boston, 1875 . . . . 4 . 325
DRAMAS. James A. Hillhouse. 2 v. 16°. Boston, 1839 . . . . . . 21 . 233–34
DRAMATIC stories. L. H. Phelps. 12°. Chicago, 1874 . . . . 21 . 223
DRAPER, John William. History of the conflict between religion and science. 12°. New York, 1875 . . . . 13 . 1123
DRAWING-ROOM (The) stage. G. M. Baker. 16°. Boston, 1874 . . . 21 . 240
DRESS-REFORM. Ed. by A. G. Woolson. 16°. Boston, 1874 . . . . . 13 . 963
DR. OX's experiments, and other stories. Jules Verne. Sq. 16°. Boston, 1875. 2 copies . . . . 4 . 1215–16
*DROLL stories. Honoré de Balzac. Sm. 8°. London, 1874 . . . . . 4 . 450
DROZ, Gustave. Around a spring. Trans. from the French by M. S. 16°. New York, 1873 . . . . 4 . 861
Babolain. A novel. Trans. from the French by M. S. 16°. New York, 1873 . . . . 4 . 862
DUDEVANT, Amantine Lucile Aurore Dupin. [*George Sand.*] My sister Jeannie. A novel. Trans. from the French by S. R. Crocker. 16°. Boston, 1874 . . . . 4 . 835

E.

EARLE, John. The philology of the English tongue. Sm. 8°. London, 1873 . . . . 13 . 868
EARNEST words on true success in life. Ray Palmer. 16°. New York and Chicago, 1873 . . . . 13 . 169
EARTH (The) as modified by human action. George P. Marsh. 8°. New York, 1874 . . . . 13 . 1306
EARTHWARD (The) pilgrimage. M. D. Conway. 16°. New York, 1874 . 13 . 160
ECHOES of the foot-hills. Bret Harte. 16°. Boston, 1875 . . . . . . 21 . 244
ECKEL, Lizzie St. John. Maria Monk's daughter; an autobiography. Portrait. Illustrated. 8°. New York, 1874 . . . . 4 . 548
ELECTIC magazine. Vols. 19 and 20, new series. 8°. New York, 1874. 19 . 630–31
ECLIPSES past and future. S. J. Johnson. Sm. 8°. Oxford and London, 1874 . . . . 13 . 859
EDITH's mistake. Jennie Woodville. (*Pseud.*) 16°. Philadelphia, 1874. 4 . 979
EDNA Browning. M. J. Holmes. 12°. New York, 1874. 2 copies. . 3 . 1343–44
EDUCATION of American girls. Ed. by Anna C. Brackett. 12°. New York, 1874 . . . . 13 . 952

Edwards, *Mrs.* Annie. Estelle. A novel. 12°. New York, 1874. 2 copies . . . . 4 . 919–20

> *Note.* — This book was published in England, under the title of "Creeds;" but at the suggestion of Mrs. Edwards it is presented in America by the name of the heroine of the story, "Estelle."

Edward's wife. Emma Marshall. 16°. New York [n. d.] . . . . . . 4 . 844
Eggleston, Edward. The circuit rider; a tale of the heroic age. Illustrated. 12°. New York, 1874 . . . . 4 . 456
Eggleston, George Cary. A rebel's recollections. 16°. New York, 1875 . . . . 4 . 578
Egypt and Iceland in the year 1874. B. Taylor. 12°. New York, 1874. 13 . 946
Egypt of the Pharaohs and of the Kedive. F. Barham Zincke. 8°. London, 1871 . . . . 13 . 1352
Ellis, Grace A. The Life and works of *Mrs.* Anna Lætitia Barbauld. 2 v. 12°. Boston, 1874 . . . . 13 . 167–68

> Vol. I. Memoir, with many of her letters.
> II. Selections from poems and prose writings.

Ellis, *Mrs.* Sarah Stickney, *formerly Miss Stickney.* The mothers of great men. Sm. 8°. London. [n. d.] . . . . 13 . 111
Elze, Karl. Essays on Shakspeare. Trans. by L. Dora Schmitz. 8°. London, 1874 . . . . 13 . 1320
Emigrant's (The) story, and other poems. J. T. Trowbridge. 16°. Boston, 1875 . . . . 21 . 246
Empty (The) heart: or, husks. M. V. Terhune. 12°. New York, 1874. 4 . 1103
*England, Baronetage of, and of such baronets of Scotland as are of English families. *Rev.* William Betham. 5 v. 4°. London and Ipswich, 1801–5 . . . . 13 . 1521–25
England, History of, from 1830–1874. William N. Molesworth. 3 v. Sm. 8°. London, 1874. . . . . 13 . 164–66
England political and social. A. Laugel. 16°. New York, 1874 . . . 13 . 949
English (The) in Ireland in the eighteenth century. J. A. Froude. 3 v. Sm. 8°. New York, 1873–74 . . . . 13 . 1120–22
English language, History of. H. E. Shepherd. 16°. New York, 1874. 13 . 1158
English literature, A first sketch of. Henry Morley. Sm. 8°. London. [n. d.] . . . . 13 . 924
English literature, History of. H. A. Taine. 4 v. 8°. Edinburgh, 1873 . . . . 13 . 1210–13
English (The) orphans. M. J. Holmes. 12°. New York, 1874. 2 copies. 3 . 1345–46
English people. The pedigree of. Thomas Nicholas. 8°. London, 1874. 13 . 1338
English and Scottish ballads. Edited by F. J. Child. 8 v. Sm. 8°. Boston, 1860 . . . . 21 . 214–21
English (Our) surnames. C. W. Bardsley. Sm. 8°. London, 1873. 13 . 153
*Engravings of the most noble the Marquis of Stafford's collection of pictures, in London; arranged according to schools, and in chronological order, with remarks on each picture, by William Young Ottley, the executive part under the management of Peltro William Tomkins. 4 v. Imp. 4°. London, 1818. . . . . 15 . 1410–13
Epistles of Lucius Annæus Seneca with large annotations. 2 v. in 1. 4°. London, 1786 . . . . 13 . 1509

EPISTLES on women. Lucy Aikin. 12°. Boston, 1810 . . . . 21 . 251
ERA (The) of the Protestant revolution. Frederic Seebohm. 16°. New York, 1874 . . . . 13 . 872
ERCKMANN, Emile, and CHATRIAN, Alexandre. The Alsacian schoolmaster. Sm. 8°. London [n. d.] . . . . 4 . 937
ESSAYS. John Foster. 12°. Philadelphia, 1844 . . . . 13 . 839
*ESSAYS on morality and natural religion. *Lord* Kames. 8°. Edinburgh, 1779 . . . . 13 . 1207
ESSAYS in a series of letters. John Foster. 12°. New York, 1847 . . . 13 . 840
ESSAYS on Shakspeare. Karl Elze. 8°. London, 1874 . . . . 13 . 1320
*ESSEX County (Mass.) Atlas, from actual surveys and official records. Compiled by D. G. Beers & Co. Roy. 4°. Philadelphia, 1872 . . 15 . 1416
ESTELLE. (A novel.) *Mrs.* Annie Edwards. 12°. New York, 1874. 2 copies . . . . 4 . 919–20
ESTES, Dana, *editor.* Half-hour recreations in popular science. By R. A. Proctor, R. Virchow, H. Schellen, Prof. Roscoe, J. N. Lockyer, J. D. Dana, Dr. Carpenter, Pres. Winchell, Prof. Huxley, J. H. Tice, E. B. Taylor, Dr. Richardson, T. Sterry Hunt, Prof. Clifford, R. Hunt, H. W. Dove, and *others.* 1st series. 8°. Boston, 1874. . 13 . 1242
ETHELYN'S mistake. M. J. Holmes. 12°. New York, 1874. 2 copies 3 . 1347–48
ETRUSCAN researches. Isaac Taylor. Sm. 8°. London, 1874 . . . . 13 . 1241
EUROPE. Pen pictures of Europe. E. Peake. 8°. Philadelphia, 1874 . 13 . 1137
EUSTACE Quentin. G. W. M. Reynolds. 8°. Philadelphia [n. d.] . . . 4 . 538
EUTHANASY; or, happy talk towards the end of life. W. Mountford. 12°. Boston, 1874 . . . . 13 . 922
EVANGELICAL alliance conference, 1873. Edited by *Rev.* P. Schaff, and *Rev.* S. I. Prime. L. 8°. New York, 1874 . . . . 13 . 1301
*EVER Green (The): being a collection of Scots poems, wrote by the ingenious before 1600. Ed. by Allan Ramsay. [Reprint.] 2 v. 12°. Glasgow, 1824 . . . . 21 . 253–54
EVOLUTION, The doctrine of. A. Winchell. 16°. New York, 1874 . . 13 . 172
EVOLUTION and progress. W. I. Gill. Sm. 8°. New York, 1875 . . . 13 . 938
EXHIBITION (The) drama: comprising drama, comedy, and farce. G. M. Baker. 16°. Boston, 1875 . . . . 21 . 241
EXPRESSMAN (The): and the detective. A. Pinkerton. 16°. Chicago, 1874. 4 . 975
EYRE, Edward John. Journals of expeditions of discovery into Central Australia, and overland from Adelaide to King George's Sound. 1840–41. 2 v. 8°. London, 1845 . . . . 13 . 1216–17

F.

FABLES in song. Robert *Lord* Lytton. 16°. Boston, 1874 . . . . . . 21 . 250
FAIR (The) maid of Perth. *Sir* W. Scott. 2 v. in 1. 12°. Boston, 1874. 4 . 219
FAIR Play. E. D. E. N. Southworth. 12°. Philadelphia, 1868 . . . . 4 . 1015
*FALL RIVER (Mass.) city directory. 1874. 8°. Fall River, 1874 . . . 11 . 1252
*FALL RIVER (Mass.) city document. No. 27. 8°. Fall River, 1874 . . 11 . 1235
FALLEN pride. E. D. E. N. Southworth. 12°. Philadelphia, 1868 . . . 4 . 1017
FAME and fortune. H. Alger, jun. 16°. Boston, 1868. 2 copies . . 4 . 1155–56

FAMILY (The) doom. E. D. E. N. Southworth. 12°. Philadelphia, 1869. 4 . 1018
FAMILY (The) scapegrace. J. Payn. Sm. 8°. London [n. d.] . . . . 4 . 569
FAR from the madding crowd. T. Hardy. 16°. New York, 1874 . . . 4 . 865
FARQUHARSON, Martha. *See* FINLEY, Martha.
FARRAR, Frederick William. The life of Christ. 2 woodcuts. 2 v. 8°. New York, 1874 . . . . 13 . 1342–43

Note. — This work was prepared by the author at the request of Messrs. Cassell, Petter, and Galpin, the English publishers. It is thoroughly evangelical in spirit, and aims to present the authentic history of the life of Christ, founded on an independent study of the four Gospels. While not unmindful of objections, difficulties, and the criticisms of sceptical writers, it is not written in a controversial style, but discusses the subject from the point of view of a sincere believer. It contains in the appendix discussions which embody the latest researches. A list of authorities is prefixed, of great value to one interested in the literature of the subject. The book has already taken high rank as an exposition of the life and character of Christ.

The silence and the voices of God, with other sermons. Sm. 8°. London, 1874 . . . . 13 . 928
FAST friends. J. T. Trowbridge. 16°. Boston, 1875. 2 copies . . . . 4 . 574–5
FAST (A) life. J. Taylor. 12°. New York, 1874 . . . . 4 . 261
FATAL (The) Marriage. E. D. E. N. Southworth. 12°. Philadelphia, 1863. 4 . 1020
FATHERS and sons. T. Hook. 16°. London [n. d.] . . . . 4 . 810
FAUNCE, Daniel Worcester. The Christian in the world. 16°. Boston, 1875. 13 . 1174
FERRIER, M. Destiny; or, the chief's daughter. 16°. London [n. d.] . 4 . 824
The inheritance. 16°. London [n. d.] . . . . 4 . 825
Marriage. 16°. London [n. d.] . . . . 4 . 826
F. GRANT & Co. G. L. Chaney. 16°. Boston, 1875 . . . . 4 . 379
FIELD, Maunsell Bradhurst. Memories of many men and some women; being personal recollections of emperors, kings, queens, princes, presidents, &c., for the last thirty years. 12°. New York, 1874 . . . 13 . 152
FIELD, (M.) Kate. Ten days in Spain. Illustrated. Sq. 16°. Boston, 1875. 13 . 977
FIELD, cover, and trap shooting. A. H. Bogardus. Sm. 8°. New York, 1874. 13 . 1149
FIELD and forest. W. T. Adams. 16°. Boston, 1875 . . . . 4 . 326
FIELD (The) of ice. *A Sequel* to A journey to the north pole. Jules Verne. Sm. 8°. New York, 1875. 2 copies . . . . 4 . 1230–31
FIGHTING fire. The great fires of history, including the conflagrations in Chicago, Boston, Portland, New York, &c. With a history of Insurance. 8°. Hartford, 1873 . . . . 13 . 1060
FIGHTING Joe. W. T. Adams. 16°. Boston, 1875 . . . . 4 . 304
FINE and ornamental arts, Lectures on the history and practice of. W. B. Scott. 16°. New York, 1875 . . . . 13 . 1170
FINLEY, Martha, *formerly Miss Farquharson.* Our Fred; or, seminary life at Thurston. 16°. New York, 1874 . . . . 4 . 828
FIRE (The) brigade. R. M. Ballantyne. 16°. Philadelphia [n. d.] . . 4 . 1202
FIRES, fire engines, and fire brigades. Charles F. T. Young. 8°. London, 1866 . . . . 13 . 1061
FISHER (The) boys of Pleasant cove. E. Kellogg. 16°. Boston, 1874 . 4 . 952
FISHING (The) tourist. Charles Hallock. 8°. New York, 1873 . . . 13 . 1244
FISKE, John. Outlines of cosmic philosophy, based on the doctrine of evolution, with criticisms on the positive philosophy. 2v. 8°. Boston, 1875 . . . . 13 . 1258–59

FITZ-PATRICK, Walter. The great Condé, and the period of the Fronde. 2 v. 8°. London, 1874 . . . . 13 . 1261–62
FIVE-MINUTE chats with young women. Dio Lewis. Sm. 8°. New York, 1874 . . . . 13 . 948
FIVE weeks in a balloon. Jules Verne. Sm. 8°. Boston, 1874. 2 copies. 4 . 1217–18
FLAG (The) of truce. Susan Warner. 16°. New York, 1875 . . . . 4 . 375
FLASHES of thought. C. H. Spurgeon. Sm. 8°. London, 1874. . . . 13 . 126
FLEMING, May Agnes. Guy Earlscourt's wife. (A novel.) 12°. New York, 1874 . . . . 4 . 1334
A terrible secret. (A novel.) 12°. New York, 1874 . . . . 4 . 1335
A wonderful woman. (A novel.) 12°. New York, 1874. . . . . . 4 . 1336
FLEURANGE. (A novel.) *Mme.* A. Craven. 16°. New York, 1873 . . 4 . 860
FLITCH (The) of bacon. W. H. Ainsworth. 16°. London [n. d.] . . . 4 . 1169
FLOATING (A) city, and The blockade runners. Jules Verne. Sq. 16°. New York. 1874 . . . . 4 . 1219
The same. Sq. 16°. New York, 1875 . . . . 4 . 1220
FLOATING (The) light of the Goodwin sands. R. M. Ballantyne. 16°. Philadelphia [n. d.] . . . . 4 . 1203
FLOOD and field. W. H. Maxwell. Sm. 8°. London [n. d.] . . . . . 4 . 429
*FLÜCKIGER, Friedrich A., and HANBURY, Daniel. Pharmacographia. A history of the principal drugs of vegetable origin met with in Great Britain and British India. 8°. London, 1874 . . . . 13 . 1550
FLY Leaves. C. S. Claverley. 16°. New York, 1872 . . . . 21 . 249
FOLLOWING the flag. C. C. Coffin. 16°. Boston, 1865. . . . . . . 4 . 257
FOOTE, *Admiral* A. H. Life of. J. M. Hoppin. 8°. New York, 1874 . 13 . 1350
FOOTE, E. B. Science in story. Sammy Tubbs, the boy doctor, and "Spousie" the troublesome monkey. 4 v. Sq. 8°. New York, 1874 . . 4 . 884–7
FOOTFALLS on the boundary of another world. R. D. Owen. 12°. Philadelphia, 1874. . . . . 13 . 1269
FOOTSTEPS to fame. J. H. Friswell. Sm 8°. London, 1874 . . . . . 13 . 159
FOR better or worse. J. C. Croly. 16°. Boston, 1875 . . . . 4 . 373
FORBES, A. Gruar. Geographical exploration and Christian enterprise in Africa. Sm. 8°. London, 1874. . . . . 13 . 1172
FORBES, J. H. [*Arthur Locker.*] On a coral reef: the story of a runaway trip to sea. Sm. 8°. London [n. d.] . . . . 4 . 838
FOREGONE (A) conclusion. W. D Howells. 16°. Boston, 1875 . . . 4 . 453
FOREST (The) and the field. H. A. Lloyd. Sm. 8°. London, 1874. . . 4 . 475
FOREST (The) exiles. M. Reid. 16°. Boston, 1874 . . . . 4 . 1244
FOREST glen series. *See* KELLOGG, Elijah.
FORESTER, Frank [*Pseud.*]. *See* HERBERT, Henry William.
*FORMULARE Anglicanum. Thomas Madox. Folio. London, 1702 . . 13 . 1505
FORREST, Edwin. Life of; with reminiscences and personal recollections. James Rees. 12°. Philadelphia, 1874 . . . . 13 . 133
FORSTER, John. Life of Charles Dickens. Portrait. Vol. 3. 12°. Philadelphia, 1874 . . . . 13 . 162
FORTUNE (The) seeker. E. D. E. N. Southworth. 12°. Philadelphia, 1866 . . . . 4 . 1021
FORTUNES (The) of Glencore. C. Lever. Sm. 8°. London, 1873 . . . 4 . 410
FORTUNES (The) of Hector O'Halloran. W. H. Maxwell. Sm. 8°. London [n. d.] . . . . 4 . 430

5

FORTUNES (The) of Nigel. *Sir* W. Scott. 2 v. in 1. 12°. Boston, 1872. 4 . 220
FOSDICK, Charles A. [*Harry Castlemon.*] *Go-ahead series.* 3 v. 16°. Cincinnati, 1868–70. Illustrated.
Tom Newcombe, or, the boy of bad habits . . . . 4 . 959
Go-ahead; or, the fisher-boy's motto . . . . 4 . 960
No moss; or, the career of a rolling stone . . . . 4 . 961

Gunboat series. Illustrated. 6 v. 16°. Cincinnati, 1865–7.
Frank the young naturalist . . . . 4 . 962
Frank in the woods . . . . 4 . 963
Frank on the prairie . . . . 4 . 964
Frank on a gunboat . . . . 4 . 965
Frank before Vicksburg . . . . 4 . 966
Frank on the Lower Mississippi . . . . 4 . 967

Rocky Mountain series. Illustrated. 3 v. 16°. Cincinnati, 1868–71.
Frank among the rancheros . . . . 4 . 968
Frank at Don Carlos' rancho . . . . 4 . 969
Frank in the mountains . . . . 4 . 970

Sportsman's club series. Illustrated. 3 v. 16°. Cincinnati, 1873–4.
The sportsman's club in the saddle . . . . 4 . 971
The sportsman's club afloat . . . . 4 . 972
The sportsman's club among the trappers . . . . 4 . 973
FOSS, Edward. Memoirs of Westminster Hall: a collection of interesting incidents, anecdotes, and historical sketches, relating to Westminster Hall, its famous judges and lawyers, and its great trials. With an historical introduction. Illustrations. 2 v. 8°. New York, 1874. 13 . 1333–34
FOSTER, John. Essays. 12°. Philadelphia, 1844 . . . . 13 . 839
Essays in a series of letters. 12°. New York, 1847 . . . . 13 . 840
FOUL play. C. Reade, and D. Boucicault. Sm. 8°. Boston, 1874 . . . 4 . 1119
FOUR (The) civilizations of the world. H. Wikoff. 12°. Philadelphia, 1874. 13 . 170
*FRANCE. GIFFORD, JOHN. History of France. 4 v. 4°. London, 1791. 13 . 1517–20
*GUIZOT, F. P. G. History of France. 3 v. Roy. 8°. London, 1872–74. 13 . 1543–45
KITCHIN, G. W. History of France, down to the year 1453. Sm. 8°. Oxford, 1873 . . . . 13 . 150
WHITEHURST, F. M. Court and social life in France, under Napoleon III. 2 v. 8°. London, 1873 . . . . 13 . 1223–24
FRANCILLON, R. E. Zelda's fortune. 8°. Boston, 1874 . . . . 4 . 531
FRANK among the rancheros. C. A. Fosdick. 16°. Cincinnati, 1871 . . . 4 . 968
FRANK at Don Carlos' rancho. C. H. Fosdick. 16°. Cincinnati, 1871 . 4 . 969
FRANK before Vicksburg. C. H. Fosdick. 16°. Cincinnati, 1867 . . . 4 . 966
FRANK in the mountains. C. A. Fosdick. 16°. Cincinnati, 1867 . . . 4 . 970
FRANK in the woods. C. A. Fosdick. 16°. Cincinnati, 1867 . . . . . 4 . 963
FRANK on a gunboat. C. A. Fosdick. 16°. Cincinnati, 1865 . . . . . 4 . 965
FRANK on the Lower Mississippi. C. A. Fosdick. 16°. Cincinnati, 1867 . . 4 . 967
FRANK on the prairie. C. A. Fosdick. 16°. Cincinnati, 1867 . . . . 4 . 964
FRANK, the young naturalist. C. A. Fosdick. 16°. Cincinnati, 1867 . . 4 . 962
FRANK Mildmay. F. Marryat. 12°. London [n. d.] . . . . 4 . 238
FRANKLIN, Benjamin. Life of, written by himself. Now first edited from original MSS., and from his printed correspondence, and other writings, by John Bigelow. 3 v. 12°. Philadelphia, 1874 . . . . . 13 . 1344–46

*FRANKLIN County (Mass.) Atlas, from surveys by F. W. Beers, G. P. Sanford, and others. Roy. 4°. New York, 1871 . . . . 15 . 1417
FRANKLIN Institute, Journal of. Vols. 67–68. 8°. Philadelphia, 1874. 17 . 463–64
FRANK'S campaign. H. Alger, jun. 16°. Boston, 1864 . . . . 4 . 1144
FREAKS of fortune. W. T. Adams. 16°. Boston, 1875 . . . . 4 . 321
FREE (A) lance in the field of life and letters. W. C. Wilkinson. 12°. New York, 1874 . . . . 13 . 1168
FRENCH (The) humorists from the twelfth to the nineteenth century. W. Besant. 8°. Boston, 1874 . . . . 13 . 1135
FRENCH (The) revolution and first empire. William O'Connor Morris. Sm. 8°. London, 1874 . . . . 13 . 131
FRESENIUS, C. Remigius. Instruction in chemical analysis. Quantitative. Edited by J. Lloyd Bullock. 8°. London, 1846 . . . . 13 . 1406
FREYTAG, Gustav. Ingraban. Trans. from the German by *Mrs.* Malcom. 16°. New York, 1873 . . . . 4 . 863
FRIEND or foe. 16°. [n. t.] . . . . 4 . 880
FRISWELL, James Hain. Footsteps to fame: a book to open other books. New edition, illustrated. Sm. 8°. London, 1874 . . . . 13 . 159
FROM my youth up. M. V. Terhune. 12°. New York, 1874. 2 copies. 4 . 1104–5
FROM the clouds to the mountains. Jules Verne. Sq. 12°. Boston, 1874. 2 copies . . . . 4 . 1221–22
FROM the earth to the moon. J. Verne. 8°. New York, 1874. 2 copies. 4 . 1223–24
FROM the Indus to the Tigris. H. W. Bellew. L. 8°. London, 1874 . . 13 . 1329
FROUDE, James Anthony. The English in Ireland in the eighteenth century. 3 v. Sm. 8°. New York, 1873–74 . . . . 13 . 1120–22
FROZEN (The) deep. W. Collins. 12°. Boston, 1875. 3 copies . 4 . 359–60–61
FULLER, S. Margaret. *See* OSSOLI, S. M. F., *marchesa d'*.
*FULLER, Thomas, *compiler.* Introductio ad prudentiam; or, directions, counsels, and cautions, tending to prudent management of affairs in common life. Sm. 8°. London, 1726 . . . . 13 . 884
FUR (The) country. Jules Verne. 8°. Boston, 1874. 2 copies . . . 4 . 1225–26
FURNESS, Helen Kate. A concordance to Shakspeare's poems: an index to every word therein contained. Roy. 8°. Philadelphia, 1874 . . 21 . 204
FUSTEL DE COULANGES, Numa Denis. The ancient city: a study on the religion, laws, and institutions of Greece and Rome. Trans. from the latest French edition by Willard Small. Sm. 8°. Boston, 1874 . . 13 . 1252

G.

GABORIAU, Emile. The clique of gold. A novel. 8°. Boston, 1874. . 4 . 527
GAIL Hamilton [*Pseud.*]. *See* DODGE, Mary Abigail.
GAIRDNER, James. The houses of Lancaster and York, with the conquest and loss of France. With five maps. Sq. 16°. Boston, 1875 . . 13 . 885
*GALERIE du Musée de France. Publiée par Filhol, graveur. Texte par Joseph Lavallee. 11 vols. 8°. Paris, 1814–28 . . . . . . 13 . 1531–41

Note. — Contains engravings of *all* the chief paintings concentrated in the Louvre by Napoleon I. before they were again dispersed; while the folio Musée Francais and Supplement do not together comprise more than 480 subjects. The 11th volume was not published until 1828, and is wanting to the generality of copies.

GAMING (The) table: its votaries and victims. A Steinmetz. 2 v. 8°. London, 1870 .13 . 1054-55
GARDNER, E. C. Homes, and how to make them. Illustrated. 16°. Boston, 1874 . . . . 13 . 874
GARRETT, Edward [*Pseud.*]. *See* MAYO, Isabella Fivy.
GEMS. King, C. W. Hand-book of engraved gems. Illustrations. 8°. London, 1866 . . . . 13 . 1254
The natural history of gems or decorative stones. 8°. London, 1867. 13 . 1255
GENESIS (The) of New-England churches. L. Bacon. 8°. N.Y., 1874 . 13 . 1248
GENTIANELLA. *Mrs.* Randolph. Sm. 8°. Philadelphia [n. d.] . . . . 4 . 1072
GERMAN universities. J. M. Hart. 12°. New York, 1874 . . . . 13 . 1272
GERMAN university life. Heinrich Steffens. 12°. Philadelphia, 1874 . . 13 . 1161
GERMANIA, its courts, camps, and people. *Baroness* Blaze de Bury. 2 v. 8°. London, 1850 . . . . 13 . 1322-23
GERMANY. KOHLRAUSCH, F. History of Germany. 8°. New York, 1873. 13 . 1313
LEWIS, C. T. A history of Germany from the earliest times. 8°. New York, 1874 . . . . 13 . 1139
MENZEL, W. History of Germany. 3 v. Sm. 8°. New York, 1871. 13 . 956-58
GERSTAECKER, Frederich. The young whaler; or, the adventures of Charles Hollberg. Illustrated. 16°. London [n. d] . . . . 4 . 380
GERVASE Skinner. T. Hook. 16°. London [n. d.] . . . . 4 . 811
*GIFFORD, John. The history of France, from the earliest times to the present important era. From the French of Velly, Villaret, Garnier, Mezeray, Daniel, and other eminent historians; with notes, critical and explanatory. 4 v. 4°. London, 1791 . . . . 13 . 1517-20
GILBERT Gurney. T. Hook. 16°. London [n. d.] . . . . 4 . 812
GILDED (The) age. S. L. Clemens, and C. D. Warner. 8°. Hartford, 1874 . . . . 4 . 546
GILL, William I. Evolution and progress: an exposition and defence. The foundation of evolution philosophically expounded, and its arguments succinctly stated; with a review of leading opponents, as Dawson and Winchell, and *quasi* opponents, as Le Conte and Carpenter. Sm. 8°. New York, 1875 . . . . 13 . 938
GILLETT, Ezra Hall. God in human thought; or, natural theology traced in literature, ancient and modern, to the time of Bishop Butler. With a closing chapter on the moral system, and an English bibliography from Spenser to Butler. 2 v. 8°. New York, 1874 . . 13 . 1420-21
The moral system, with an historical and critical introduction. Sm. 8° New York, 1874 . . . . 13 . 1140
GILLMORE, PARKER. [*Ubique.*] Prairie and forest: a description of the game of North America, with personal adventures in their pursuits. Illustrated. 12°. New York, 1874 . . . . 13 . 1152
*GILLRAY, James. Works of, with history of his life and times. Over 400 illustrations. Ed. by Thomas Wright. Roy. 4°. London [n. d.] . 13 . 1515
GILMAN, Arthur. Seven historic ages; or, talks about kings, queens, and barbarians. Illustrated. 16°. New York, 1874 . . . . 13 . 975
GILMORE, John. Storm warriors; or, life-boat work on the Goodwin sands. Sm. 8°. London, 1874 . . . . 13 . 120
GIPSY'S [The] prophecy. E. D. E. N. Southworth. 12°. Philadelphia, 1861 . . . . 4 . 1022

GIRAFFE-hunters (The). M. Reid. 16°. Boston, 1873 . . . . 4 . 1245
GIRARDIN, *Mme.* E. de. *and others.* The cross of Berny; or, Irene's lovers. 12°. Philadelphia, 1873. 2 copies . . . . 4 . 911–12
GIRLHOOD (The) of Shakspeare's heroines; in a series of tales. M. C. Clarke Sq. 8°. New York, 1873 . . . . 4 . 804
GLAZIER, Willard. Three years in the federal cavalry. Illustrated. Sm. 8°. New York, 1874 . . . . 13 . 1153
GO-AHEAD. C. A. Fosdick. 16°. Cincinnati, 1869 . . . . 4 . 960
GOD in human thought. E. H. Gillett. 2 v. 8°. New York, 1874 . 13 . 1420–21
GOETHE, Conversations of, with Eckermann and Soret. Trans. by J. Oxenford. Sm. 8°. London, 1874 . . . . 13 . 112
GOLD-HUNTERS' (The) adventures. W. H. Thomes. 12°. Boston, 1874 . 4 . 1131
GOLD-HUNTERS (The) in Europe. W. H. Thomes. 12°. Boston, 1874 . 4 . 1133
GOODWIN, *Rev.* T. A. The mode of man's immortality; or, the when, where, and how of the future life. 12°. New York, 1874 . . . . 13 . 145
GOULD, Jeanie T. Marjorie's quest. Illustrated. 16°. Boston, 1875 . 4 . 559
*GRAMMAR. Maetzner's English Grammar, methodical, analytical, and historical. Trans. from the German by C. J. Grece. 3 v. 8°. London and Boston, 1874 . . . . 13 . 1551–53
*GRAMMAR of painting and engraving. Charles Blanc. 4°. New York, 1874 . . . . 13 . 1548
GRANT, James Augustus. A walk across Africa; or, domestic scenes from my Nile journal. 8°. Edinburgh and London, 1864 . . . . . 13 . 1219
GREAT Britain, Observations on the popular antiquities of. By John Brand; revised and enlarged by *Sir* Henry Ellis. 3 v. Sm. 8°. London, 1873 . . . . 13 . 106–8
GREAT (The) Condé and the period of Fronde. Walter Fitz-Patrick. 2 v. 8°. London, 1874 . . . . 13 . 1261–62
GREAT (The) conversers. W. Mathews. 8°. Chicago, 1874 . . . . . 13 . 122
GREAT expectations. C. Dickens. 12°. Boston, 1874 . . . . 4 . 1314
GREECE. Curtius, Ernst. History of Greece. Trans. by A. W. Ward. 5 v. 12°. New York, 1874 . . . . 13 . 1127–31
GREEN, Beriah. Miscellaneous writings. 12°. Whitesboro, 1841 . . . 13 . 854
GREEN, Henry. Shakspeare and the emblem writers; an exposition of their similarities of thought and expression. Préceded by a view of emblem-literature down to A. D. 1616. With numerous illustrative devices from the original authors. Roy. 8°. London, 1870 . . . 21 . 205
GREEN, J. R. A short history of the English people, from A. D. 449 to 1874. Maps and tables. Sm. 8°. London, 1874 . . . . 13 . 1163
GREENLEAF, Simon. The testimony of the evangelists examined by the rules of evidence administered in courts of justice. With an appendix containing a history of the most ancient manuscript copies of the New Testament, and a comparison of their text with that of the King James' Bible, by Constantine Tischendorff; also a review of the trial of Jesus. L. 8°. New York, 1874 . . . . 13 . 1307
GREVILLE, Charles Cavendish Fulke. The Greville memoirs. A journal of the reigns of King George IV. and King William IV. Edited by Henry Reeve. 3 v. 8°. London, 1874 . . . . 13 . 1050–52
GRIFFITH Gaunt. C. Reade. Sm. 8°. Boston, 1875. 2 copies . . . 4 . 1120–21
GUEST, Edwin. A history of English rhythms. 2 v. 8°. Lond., 1838. 13 . 1426–27

*GUICCIARDINI, Franc. The historie of Guicciardin; containing the warres of Italie and other partes. Reduced into English by Geffray Fenton. Folio. London, 1599 . . . . 13 . 1513
GUILD, Curtis. Over the ocean; or, sights and scenes in foreign lands. 8°. Boston, 1875 . . . . 13 . 1250
GUINNARD, A. Three years' slavery among the Patagonians. Trans. from the third French edition, by C. S. Cheltnam. 8°. London, 1871 . 13 . 143
*GUIZOT, Francois Pierre Guillaume. The history of France from the earliest times to the year 1789. Trans. by Robert Black. 3 v. Roy. 8°. London, 1872–74 . . . . 13 . 1543–45
GUNNAR: a tale of Norse life. H. H. Boyesen. Sq. 16°. Boston, 1874 . 4 . 888
GURNEY married. *A sequel* to Gilbert Gurney. T. Hook. 16°. London [n. d.] . . . . 4 . 813
GUY Earlscourt's wife. M. A. Fleming. 12°. New York, 1874 . . . . 4 . 1334
GUY Fawkes. W. H. Ainsworth. 16°. London [n. d.] . . . . 4 . 1170
GUY Mannering. *Sir* W. Scott. 2 v. in 1. 12°. Boston, 1874 . . . . 4 . 221
GWYNNE, Talbot. Young Singleton. 16°. London [n. d.] . . . . . 4 . 845

H.

HALE, Edward Everett. In His name; a story of the Waldenses, seven hundred years ago. Sq. 16°. Boston, 1874 . . . . 13 . 976
Our new crusade; a temperance story. Sq. 16°. Boston, 1875. . . 4 . 882
and others. Workingmen's homes. Essays and stories on the homes of men who work in large towns. 16°. Boston, 1874 . . . . 13 . 177
*HALES, *Rev.* William. A new analysis of chronology and geography, history and prophecy; in which their elements are attempted to be explained, harmonized, and vindicated upon scriptural and scientific principles. 4 v. 8°. London, 1830 . . . . 13 . 1554–57

Vol. I. Chronology and geography.
II. Chronological history of the Old Testament and the Apocrypha.
III. Chronological history of the New Testament.
IV. A new analysis of profane chronology.

HALF-HOUR recreations in popular science, Selected and edited by Dana Estes. 1st series. 8°. Boston, 1874 . . . . 13 . 1242
HALL, Newman. The land of the Forum and the Vatican; or, thoughts and sketches during an Easter pilgrimage to Rome. 1 plate. 16°. New York [n. d.] . . . . 13 . 1178
HALL, Theresa Oakey. Her mother's Fancy: a story for juveniles and young old folk. Sm. 8°. Boston, 1875 . . . . 4 . 562
HALLOCK, Charles. The fishing tourist. 8°. New York, 1873 . . . . 13 . 1244
HALLOWELL, Sarah Catherine. Bee's bedtime; being stories from "The Christian Union," by *Mrs.* Joshua L. Hallowell. Sm. 8°. Philadelphia, 1873. . . . . 4 . 467
HAMERTON, Eugenie. The mirror of truth, and other marvellous histories. 8 illustrations. (Juvenile.) 16°. Boston, 1875 . . . . 4 . 568
HAMILTON, Gail [*Pseud.*]. *See* DODGE, Mary Abigail.
*HAMPDEN County (Mass.) Atlas. From surveys by F. W. Beers, G. P. Sanford, and others. Roy. 4°. New York, 1870 . . . . 15 . 1418

*Hampshire County (Mass.) Atlas. From surveys under the direction of F. W. Beers. Roy. 4°. New York, 1873. . . . . 15 . 1419

Hampson, R. T. Medii ævi kalendarium; or, dates, charters, and customs of the middle ages, with kalendars from the tenth to the fifteenth century, and an alphabetical digest of obsolete names of days; forming a glossary of the dates of the middle ages, with tables and other aids for ascertaining dates. Plates. 2 v. 8°. London, 1841 . . . 13 . 1214–15

Hand-book of politics for 1874. E. McPherson. 8°. Washington, 1874. 13 . 1411

Hard cash. C. Reade. Sm. 8°. Boston, 1874 . . . . 4 . 1122

Hard-scrabble (The) of Elm-island. E. Kellogg. 16°. Boston, 1875 . 4 . 945

Hardy, Thomas. Desperate remedies. 16°. New York, 1874 . . . . 4 . 864

Far from the madding crowd. 16°. New York, 1874 . . . . 4 . 865

Under the greenwood tree. 16°. New York, 1874 . . . . 4 . 866

Harland, Marion [*Pseud.*]. *See* Terhune, Mary Virginia.

Harper's monthly magazine. Vols. 48–49. 8°. New York, 1874 . . 12 . 101-2

Harry Lorrequer. C. Lever. Sm. 8°. London, 1873 . . . . 4 . 411

Hart, James Morgan. German universities: a narrative of personal experience, with recent statistical information, practical suggestions, and a comparison of the German, English, and American systems of higher education. 12°. New York, 1874 . . . . 13 . 1272

Note. — Mr. Hart's department was law, his university Göttingen, his time 1861, &c. His book, divided nearly equally between his personal experiences as a student, and his generalizations upon his subject, gives a clear idea of the routine and accomplishments of a German student's university life, and exhibits the grounds of his own partiality for the German system.

Harte (Francis) Bret. Echoes of the foot-hills. 16°. Boston, 1875 . . 21 . 244

Mrs. Skaggs's husbands, and other sketches. 16°. Boston, 1874 . . 4 . 473

Hartwig, George. The sea and its living wonders. A popular account of the marvels of the deep, and of the progress of maritime discovery from the earliest ages to the present time. With numerous woodcuts and 8 chromoxylographic plates. 8°. London, 1873 . . . . 13 . 1318

The tropical world: aspects of man and nature in the equatorial regions of the globe. With 8 chromoxylographic plates and numerous wood-cuts. 8°. London, 1873 . . . . 13 . 1319

Haste and waste. W. T. Adams. 16°. Boston, 1875 . . . . 4 . 337

Hathaway, W. E. Christopher Crooked. A Christmas story. Illustrated. 16°. New York, 1873 . . . . 4 . 843

Haunted (The) homestead. E. D. E. N. Southworth. 12°. Philadelphia, 1860 . . . . 4 . 1023

Havelock, *General* Henry, Life of. J. T. Headley. 12°. New York, 1854 . . . . 13 . 951

Haweis, H. R. Pet; or, pastimes and penalties. (Juvenile.) Illustrated. 12°. New York, 1874 . . . . 4 . 566

Hayden, F. V. U. S. geological survey of Montana and adjacent territories. 8°. Washington, 1873 . . . . 11 . 749

U. S. geological survey of Nebraska. 8°. Washington, 1872 . . . 11 . 750

Hazel-blossoms. J. G. Whittier. 16°. Boston, 1875 . . . . 21 . 243

Hazlitt, W. Carew. Mary and Charles Lamb: poems, letters, and remains. Sm. 8°. London, 1874 . . . . 13 . 118

HEADLESS (The) horseman. M. Reid. 12°. New York, 1874 . . . . . 4 . 1246
HEADLEY, J. T. Life of *Gen.* H. Havelock. Illustrated. 12°. New York, 1854 . . . . 13 . 951
HEADSMAN (The). J. F. Cooper. 12°. New York, 1873 . . . . 4 . 1047
HEALTH and education. C. Kingsley. 12°. New York, 1874 . . . . . 13 . 101
HEART (The) of Mid-Lothian. *Sir* W. Scott. 2 v. in 1. 12°. Boston, 1874 . . . . 4 . 222
HEATON, *Mrs.* Charles. A concise history of painting. Sm. 8°. London, 1873 . . . . 13 . 925
HEAVEN, The expanse of. R. A. Proctor. 12°. New York, 1874 . . . 13 . 929
HEBBERD, S. S. The secret of Christianity. 16°. Boston, 1874 . . . 13 . 154
HEBREW history. *Rev.* Henry Cowles. 12°. New York, 1875 . . . . 13 . 1263
HEIDENMAUER (The). J. F Cooper. 12°. New York, 1873 . . . . 4 . 1048
HEINE, Heinrich. Scintillations from the prose works of. Trans. from the German by S. A. Stern. 16°. New York, 1873 . . . . 4 . 867
HEIR (The) of Marleward; or, restored. By the author of "Son and heir." 8°. Philadelphia, 1874 . . . . 4 . 529
HELEN Gardner's wedding-day. M. V. Terhune. 12°. New York, 1873 . 2 copies . . . . 4 . 1106–7
HELLWALD, Frederich von. The Russians in Central Asia. A critical examination down to the present time of the geography and history of Central Asia. Trans. from the German, by Theodore Wirgman. With a map. Sm. 8°. London, 1874 . . . . 13 . 1235
HELPS, *Sir* Arthur. Ivan de Biron; or, the Russian court in the middle of the last century. 12°. Boston, 1874 . . . . 4 . 255
Life and labors of Thomas Brassey. 1805–1870. Portrait. 8°. Boston, 1874 . . . . 13 . 1355
HER mother's fancy. T. O. Hall. Sm. 8°. Boston, 1875 . . . . 4 . 562
HERBERT, Henry William. [*Frank Forester.*] Hints to horsekeepers: a complete manual for horsemen; and chapters on mules and ponies. Illustrated. 12°. New York, 1859 . . . . 13 . 1142
HERO Carthew. L. Parr. 16°. New York, 1873 . . . . 4 . 870
HEROES (The); or, Greek fairy tales. Charles Kingsley. Sm. 8°. London, 1873 . . . . 4 . 459
HEYSE, Paul (Johann Ludwig). The maiden of Treppi; or, love's victory. From the German. 16°. New York, 1874 . . . . 4 . 830
HIDDEN (The) path. M. V. Terhune. 12°. New York, 1874 . . . . . 4 . 1108
HIGHER schools and universities in Germany. M. Arnold. Sm. 8°. London, 1874 . . . . 13 . 123
HILLHOUSE, James A. Dramas, discourses, and other pieces. 2 v. 16°. Boston, 1839 . . . . 21 . 233–34

Contents. — Vol. I. Demetria; Hadad; Percy's masque. Vol. II. The judgment; Sachem's wood; Discourses, 1. On the choice of an era in epic and tragic writing; 2. On the relations of literature to a republican government; 3. On the life and services of Lafayette; The hermit of Warkworth, by Thomas Percy.

HINTON, Howard. My comrade's adventures in the highlands, and legends of the neutral ground. Illustrated. Sm. 8°. New York, 1874. 2 copies . . . . 4 . 915–16
HINTON, James, *editor.* Physiology for practical use. With an introduction by E. L. Youmans. Sm. 8°. New York, 1874 . . . . 13 . 1266

HIS two wives. M. C. Ames. 12°. New York, 1874. 2 copies . . . 4 . 921–22
HISLOP, Alexander, *editor*. The book of Scottish anecdote. 8°. Edinburgh, 1874 . . . . 4 . 974
HISTORICAL illustrations of the Old Testament. *Rev.* G. Rawlinson. 16°. Boston, 1873 . . . . 13 . 1173
HISTORICAL notices of events in the reign of Charles I. Nehemiah Wallington. 2 v. Sm. 8°. London, 1869 . . . . 13 . 148–49
*HISTORIE of Guicciardin, containing the warres of Italie, &c. Folio. London, 1599 . . . . 13 . 1513
HISTORY of the town of Abington, Mass. Benjamin Hobart. 12°. Boston, 1866 . . . . 13 . 920
HISTORY of American currency. W. G. Sumner. 12° New York, 1874 . 13 . 933
HISTORY of the conflict between religion and science. J. W. Draper. 12°. New York, 1875 . . . . 13 . 1123
HISTORY of England from 1830–1874. William N. Molesworth. 3 v. Sm. 8°. London, 1874 . . . . 13 . 164–66
HISTORY of the English language. H. E. Shepherd. 16°. New York, 1874. . . . . 13 . 1158
HISTORY of English rhythms. E. Guest. 2 v. 8°. London, 1838 . 13 . 1426–27
*HISTORY of France. John Gifford. 4 v. 4°. London, 1791 . . 13 . 1517–20
*HISTORY of France. F. P. G. Guizot. 3 v. Roy. 8°. London, 1872–74.13 . 1543–45
HISTORY of France down to the year 1453. G. W. Kitchin. Sm. 8°. Oxford, 1873. . . . . 13 . 150
HISTORY of Germany. C. T. Lewis. 8°. New York, 1874 . . . . . 13 . 1139
HISTORY of Germany. W. Menzel. 3 v. Sm. 8°. London, 1871 . . 13 . 956–58
HISTORY of Germany. F. Kohlrausch. 8°. New York, 1873 . . . . 13 . 1313
HISTORY of Greece. Ernst Curtius. 5 v. 12°. New York, 1874 . 13 . 1127–31
HISTORY of the Inquisition. W. H. Rule. 2 v. 8°. New York, 1874. 13 . 1062–63
HISTORY of Ireland. J. A. Froude. 3 v. Sm. 8°. New York, 1873–74. 13 . 1120–22
HISTORY of the life-boat. R. Lewis. Sm. 8°. London, 1874 . . . . . 13 . 1146
HISTORY of merchant shipping and ancient commerce. W. S. Lindsay. 2 v. 8°. London, 1874 . . . . 13 . 1335–36
HISTORY of Peter the Great. J. Abbott. 16°. New York, 1874 . . . 13 . 878
HISTORY of the rise and fall of the slave-power in America. Henry Wilson. 2 v. Roy 8°. Boston, 1875 . . . . 13 . 1414–15
HISTORY of the United States, vol. 10. From 1778 to 1782. George Bancroft. 8°. Boston, 1874 . . . . 20 . 1228
HITTELL, John S. A brief history of culture. Sm. 8°. New York, 1875. 13 . 943
HOBART, Benjamin. History of the town of Abington, Mass. 12°. Boston, 1866. . . . . 13 . 920
HOLDEN with the cords. Julia L. M. Woodruff. 12°. New York, 1874 . 4 . 451
HOLLAND, Josiah Gilbert. The mistress of the manse. 16°. New York, 1874. 21 . 224
HOLLEY, Marietta. My opinions and Betsey Bobbet's. By Josiah Allen's wife. Illustrated. 12°. Hartford, 1874. 2 copies . . . . . . 4 . 901–2
HOLMES, Mary J. The Cameron pride; or, purified by suffering. 12°. New York, 1874. 2 copies . . . . 3 . 1335–6
 Cousin Maude and Rosamond. 12°. New York, 1874 2 copies. 3 . 1337–8
 Darkness and daylight. 12°. New York, 1874. 2 copies . . . 3 . 1339–40
 Dora Deane; or, the East India uncle: and Maggie Miller; or, old Hagar's secret. 12°. New York, 1874. 2 copies . . . . . . 3 . 1341–2

Holmes, Mary J. (*continued*).
Edna Browning; or, the Leighton homestead. 12°. New York, 1874. 2 copies . . . . 3 . 1343–4
The English orphans; or, a home in the new world. 12°. New York, 1874. 2 copies . . . . 3 . 1345–6
Ethelyn's mistake; or, the home in the west. 12°. New York, 1874. 2 copies . . . . 3 . 1347–8
The homestead on the hillside, and other tales. 12°. New York, 1874. 2 copies . . . . 3 . 1349–50
Hugh Worthington. 12°. New York, 1874. 2 copies . . . . 3 . 1351–2
Lena Rivers. 12°. New York, 1874. 2 copies . . . . 3 . 1353–4
Marian Grey; or, the heiress of Redstone Hall. 12°. New York, 1874. 2 copies . . . . 3 . 1355–6
Meadow-brook. 12°. New York, 1874. 2 copies . . . . 3 . 1357–8
Millbank; or, Roger Irving's ward. 12°. New York, 1874. 2 copies. 3 . 1359–60
Rose Mather. 12°. New York, 1874. 2 copies . . . . 3 . 1361–2
Tempest and Sunshine; or, life in Kentucky. 12°. New York, 1874. 2 copies . . . . 3 . 1363–4
West lawn; and The rector of St. Mark's. 12°. New York, 1874. 2 copies . . . . 3 . 1365–6
Holmes, Oliver Wendell. Songs of many seasons. 1862–74. 16°. Boston, 1875 . . . . 21 . 245
Home as found. J. F. Cooper. 12°. New York, 1873 . . . . 4 . 1050
Home memories. *Mrs.* Carey Brock. 16°. New York [n. d.] . . . . 4 . 378
Homes and how to make them. E. C. Gardner. 16°. Boston, 1874 . . 13 . 874
Homestead (The) on the hillside. M. J. Holmes. 12°. New York, 1874. 2 copies . . . . 3 . 1349–50
Homeward bound. J. F. Cooper. 12°. New York, 1873 . . . . 4 . 1049
Honest John Vane. J. W. De Forest. 16°. New York, 1875 . . . . 4 . 936
Hook, Theodore (Edward). All in the wrong. 16°. London [n. d.] . . 4 . 807
Cousin Geoffry. 16°. London [n. d.] . . . . 4 . 808
Cousin William; or, the fatal attachment. 16°. London [n. d.] . . 4 . 809
Fathers and sons. 16°. London [n. d.] . . . . 4 . 810
Gervase Skinner; or, the sin of economy. 16°. London [n. d.] . . 4 . 811
Gilbert Gurney. 16°. London [n. d.] . . . . 4 . 812
Gurney married. *A sequel* to Gilbert Gurney. 16°. London [n. d.] . 4 . 813
Jack Brag. 16°. London, 1872 . . . . 4 . 814
The man of many friends, and the friend of the family. 16°. London [n. d.] . . . . 4 . 815
Maxwell. 16°. London [n. d.] . . . . 4 . 816
Merton; or, "There's many a slip 'twixt the cup and the lip." 16°. London [n. d.] . . . . 4 . 817
The parson's daughter. 16°. London [n. d.] . . . . 4 . 818
Passion and principle. 16°. London [n. d.] . . . . 4 . 819
Peregrine Bunce; or, settled at last. 16°. London [n. d.] . . . . 4 . 820
The widow and the marquess; or, love and pride. 16°. London [n. d.] 4 . 821
Hooper, Henry. The lost model. 12°. Philadelphia, 1874 . . . . . 4 . 254
Hope, F. T. L. The three homes: a tale for fathers and sons. Illustrated. 12°. New York [n. d.] . . . . 4 . 462
Hope and have. W. T. Adams. 16°. Boston, 1875 . . . . 4 . 336

HOPKINS, Mark. Prayer and the prayer gauge. 16°. New York [n. d.] . . . . 13 . 175
Strength and beauty: discussions for young men. 16°. New York, 1874 . . . . 13 . 1166
HOPPIN, James Mason. Life of Andrew Hull Foote, Rear-Admiral United States Navy. Portrait and illustrations. 8°. New York, 1874 . . 13 . 1350
HORÆ Hellenicæ: essays on points of Greek philology and antiquity. John S. Blackie. 8°. London, 1874 . . . . 13 . 1064
HORSEKEEPERS, Hints to. H. W. Herbert. 12°. New York, 1859 . . . 13 . 1142
HORTON, Caroline W. Architecture for general students. With descriptive illustrations. 16°. New York, 1874 . . . . 13 . 962
HOSACK, John. Mary Queen of Scots, and her accusers; embracing a narrative of events from the death of James V. in 1542 until the death of the Regent Murray in 1570. 8°. Edinburgh and London, 1869 . . 13 . 1222
HOTTEN, John Camden, *editor*. Abyssinia and its people; or, life in the land of Prester John. With a new map and eight colored illustrations. Sm. 8°. London, 1868 . . . . 13 . 931
* The original lists of persons of quality, emigrants, religious exiles, political rebels, serving-men sold for a term of years, apprentices, children stolen, maidens pressed, and others who went from Great Britain to the American plantations, 1600–1700, with their ages, the localities where they formerly lived in the mother country, the names of the ships in which they embarked, and other interesting particulars; from MSS. preserved in the State paper department of her Majesty's public record office, England. 4°. London, 1874 . . . . 13 . 1546
HOUSES (The) of Lancaster and York. J. Gairdner. Sq. 16°. Boston, 1875 . . . . 13 . 885
How he won her. E. D. E. N. Southworth. 12°. Philadelphia, 1869 . . 4 . 1016
How Marjory helped. M. Caroll. 16°. Boston, 1874 . . . . 4 . 567
HOWE, Cupples. The deserted ship: a real story of the Atlantic. Illustrated. Sm. 8°. London, 1873 . . . . 4 . 875
HOWE, Joseph W. The breath, and the diseases which give it a fetid odor, with directions for treatment. 12°. New York, 1874. . . . 13 . 940
Winter homes for invalids: an account of the various localities in Europe and America, suitable for consumptives and other invalids during the winter months, with special reference to the climatic variations at each place, and their influence on disease. Sm. 8°. New York, 1875 . . . . 13 . 941
HOWE, Julia Ward. Sex and education: a reply to *Dr.* E. H. Clarke's "Sex in education." 16°. Boston, 1873. . . . . 13 . 863
HOWELLS, William Dean. A foregone conclusion. 16°. Boston, 1875 . 4 . 453
HÜBNER, Joseph Alexander von. A ramble round the world, 1871. Trans. by Lady Herbert. 8°. New York, 1874 . . . . 13 . 932
HUEFFER, Franz. Richard Wagner and the music of the future. History and æsthetics. 8°. London, 1874 . . . . 13 . 1239
HUGESSEN, Edward Hugessen Knatchbull. *See* KNATCHBULL-Hugessen, E. H.
HUGH Worthington. M. J. Holmes. 12°. New York, 1874. 2 copies . 3 . 1351–52
HUGO, Victor (Marie), *vicomte*. Ninety-three. Trans. by Frank Lee Benedict. Sm. 8°. New York, 1874 . . . . 4 . 449

HUGO, Victor (Marie) *vicomte* (*continued*).
The Rhine: a tour from Paris to Mayence by the way of Aix-la-Chapelle. With an account of its legends, antiquities, and important historical events. Trans. by D. M. Aird. 16°. Boston [n. d.] . . 13 . 161
HUGUENOTS (The) in France. S. Smiles. Sm. 8°. New York, 1874 . . 13 . 1237
HULDA; or, the deliverer. F. Lewald. 12°. Philadelphia, 1874. 2 copies. 3 . 1367–68
HUMAN longevity: its facts and its fictions. W. J. Thoms. Sm. 8°. London, 1873 . . . . 13 . 844
HUMAN nature, A treatise on. David Hume. 2 v. Roy. 8°. London, 1874 . . . . 13 . 1416–17
HUMAN physiology, Principles of. W. B. Carpenter. 8°. Philadelphia, 1847 . . . . 13 . 1425
HUME, Abraham. The learned societies and printing clubs of the United Kingdom: being an account of their respective origin, history, objects, and constitution; and a general introduction and a classified index. Compiled from official documents. With a supplement containing all the recently-established societies and printing clubs, and their publications to the present time. By A. J. Evans. Sm. 8°. London, 1853 . . . . 13 . 151
HUME, David. A treatise on human nature; being an attempt to introduce the experimental method of reasoning into moral subjects and dialogues concerning natural religion. Edited with preliminary dissertations and notes by T. H. Green, and T. H. Grose. 2 v. Roy. 8°. London, 1874 . . . . 13 . 1416–17
HUNDRED (A) ministers, and how they switched off. Some account of the lights and shadows of ministerial life. 16°. Boston, 1874 . . . . 4 . 841
HUNT, Thomas Sterry. Chemical and geological essays. 8°. Boston, 1875 . . . . 13 . 1132
HUNTER (The) and trapper in North America. B. Révoil. 16°. London, 1874. 2 copies . . . . 4 . 925–26
HUNTER'S (The) feast. M. Reid. 12°. New York, 1874 . . . . . . 4 . 1247
HURST, John F. Life and literature in the fatherland. 8°. New York, 1875 . . . . 13 . 1136
HUSBANDS and homes. M. V. Terhune. 12°. New York, 1874 . . . . 4 . 1109
HUTCHINSON, Thomas Joseph. Two years in Peru, with explorations of its antiquities. With a map by Daniel Barrera, and numerous illustrations. 2 v. 8°. London, 1873 . . . . 13 . 1225–26

I.

* ILLUSTRIOUS literary characters, A gallery of. (1830–38.) Drawn by the late Daniel Maclise, and accompanied by notices chiefly by the late William Maginn. Ed. by William Bates. 4°. London [n. d.] . . 13 . 1514
ILLUSTRIOUS soldiers, Sketches of. J. G. Wilson. 12°. New York, 1874. 13 . 954
IN His name. E. E. Hale. Sq. 16°. Boston, 1874 . . . . 13 . 976
IN school and out. W. T. Adams. 16°. Boston, 1875 . . . . 4 . 333
IN search of the castaways. Jules Verne. 8°. Philadelphia, 1874. 2 copies. 4 . 1235–36
IN the wilds of Africa. W. H. G. Kingston. 8°. London, 1872 . . . . 4 . 931

INDIA; or, the pearl of Pearl River. E. D. E. N. Southworth. 12°. Philadelphia, 1857 . . . . 4 . 1024
INDIAN (The) question. F. A. Walker. 12°. Boston, 1874 . . . . . . 13 . 857
INGRABAN. (A novel.) G. Freytag. 16°. New York, 1873 . . . . . . 4 . 863
INHERITANCE (The). M. Ferrier. 16°. London [n. d.] . . . . 4 . 825
INQUISITION, History of the. W. H. Rule. 2 v. 8°. New York, 1874. 13 . 1062–63
INTERNATIONAL scientific series; *namely*, —
COOKE, JOSIAH P. The new chemistry. Sm. 8°. New York, 1874 . 13 . 1154
DRAPER, JOHN W. History of the conflict between religion and science. Sm. 8°. New York, 1874 . . . . 13 . 1123
MAREY, E. J. Animal mechanism: a treatise on terrestrial and aërial locomotion. Sm. 8°. New York, 1874 . . . . 13 . 1143
MAUDSLEY, HENRY. Responsibility in mental disease. Sm. 8°. New York, 1874 . . . . 13 . 130
STEWART, BALFOUR. The conservation of energy. Sm. 8°. New York, 1874 . . . . 13 . 136
IRELAND. Froude, J. A. The English in Ireland in the eighteenth century. 3 v. Sm. 8°. New York, 1874 . . . . 13 . 1120–22
IRENE; or, beach-broken billows. *Mrs.* B. F. Baer. 16°. New York, 1875. 4 . 461
IRON (The) horse. R. M. Ballantyne. Sm. 8°. London, 1872 . . . . 4 . 1204
ISMAILIA: a narrative of the expedition to Central Africa. Organized by Ismail, Khedive of Egypt. *Sir* S. W. Baker. L. 8°. New York, 1875. 13 . 1315
IT is never too late to mend. C. Reade. Sm. 8°. Boston, 1874 . . . . 4 . 1124
ITALIAN (The) girl. Katherine S. Washburne. 12°. Boston, 1874 . . 4 . 479
IVAN de Biron. *Sir* Arthur Helps. 12°. Boston, 1874 . . . . 4 . 255
IVANHOE. *Sir* W. Scott. 2 v. in 1. 12°. Boston, 1874 . . . . 4 . 223

J.

JACK Adams. W. James. 12°. London [n. d.] . . . . 4 . 435
JACK Brag. T. Hook. 16°. London, 1872 . . . . 4 . 814
JACK Hazard and his fortunes. J. T. Trowbridge. 16°. Boston, 1873 . 4 . 576
JACK Hinton. C. Lever. Sm. 8°. London [n. d.], ... 4 . 412
JACK Sheppard. W. H. Ainsworth. 16°. London [n. d.] . . . . 4 . 1171
JACK Tier. J. F. Cooper. 12°. New York, 1873 . . . . 4 . 1051
JACOB Faithful. F. Marryat. 12°. London, 1873 . . . . 4 . 239
JAMES, *Mrs.* Edwin. Social fetters. Sm. 8°. London, 1869 . . . . . 4 . 564
JAMES, George Payne Rainsford. A book of the passions. Illustrated with 16 engravings. 8°. London, 1839 . . . . 13 . 1231
JAMES, William. [*Capt. Chamier.*] Ben Brace, the last of Nelson's Agamemnons. 12°. London [n. d.] . . . . 4 . 434
Jack Adams; or, the mutiny of the Bounty. 12°. London [n. d.] . . 4 . 435
The life of a sailor. 12°. London [n. d.] . . . . 4 . 436
Tom Bowling. 12°. London [n. d.] . . . . 4 . 437
JAMES the second. An historical romance. W. H. Ainsworth. 16°. London [n. d.] . . . . 4 . 1172
JAMIESON, Robert, *editor*. Popular ballads and songs from tradition, manuscripts, and scarce editions; with translations from the ancient Danish language, and a few originals by the editor. 2 v. 8°. Edinburgh, 1806 . . . . 21 . 211–12

JAPHET in search of a father. F. Marryat. 12°. London, 1873 . . . . 4 . 240
JAY, W. M. L. [*Pseud.*]. *See* WOODRUFF, Julia Louisa Matilda.
JEFFERSON, Thomas, Life of. J. Parton. 8°. Boston, 1874 . . . . . . 13 . 1249
JENKINS, *Mrs.* C. Jupiter's daughters. A novel. 16°. New York, 1874 . 4 . 868
—— "Who breaks — pays." ("Chi rompe — paga," Italian proverb.) 16°. New York, 1873 . . . . 4 . 869
JENNINGS, Hargrave. Live lights or dead lights. (Altar or table?) Sm. 8°. London, 1873 . . . . 13 . 115
JESSAMINE. M. V. Terhune. 12°. New York, 1874 . . . . 4 . 1110
JESSUP, *Rev.* Henry H. Syrian home-life. *Compiled by Rev.* Isaac Riley. Illustrated. 16°. New York, 1874 . . . . 13 . 124
The women of the Arabs. With a chapter for children. Edited by C. S. Robinson and Isaac Riley. 12°. New York, 1873 . . . . 13 . 125
JOHN, Eugenie. The second wife: a romance. From the German of E. Marlitt [*pseud.*], by *Mrs.* A. L. Wister. 12°. Philadelphia, 1874 . 4 . 1142
JOHN Godsoe's legacy. E. Kellogg. 16°. Boston, 1874 . . . . 4 . 951
JOHN Worthington's name. F. L. Benedict. 8°. New York, 1874 . . . 4 . 524
JOHNSON, Rossiter, *editor.* Little classics. Vol. I. Exile. Sq. 16°. Boston, 1875 . . . . 13 . 887–90

Contents. — Vol. I. Ethan Brand, by N. Hawthorne; The swans of Lir, by G. Griffin; A night in a workhouse, by J. Greenwood; The outcasts of Poker Flat, by Bret Harte; The man without a country, by E. E. Hale; The flight of a Tartar tribe, by T. De Quincey.

Same. Vol. II. Intellect. Sq. 16°. Boston, 1875. 13 . 888

Contents. — Vol. II. The house and the brain, by E. Bulwer-Lytton; D'outre mort, by Harriet P. Spofford; The fall of the house of Usher, by E. A. Poe; Chops the dwarf, by C. Dickens; Wakefield, by N. Hawthorne; Murder, considered as one of the fine arts, by T. De Quincey; The captain's story, by Rebecca H. Davis.

Same. Vol. III. Tragedy. Sq. 16°. Boston, 1875. 13 . 889

Contents. — Vol. III. The murders in the Rue Morgue, by E. A. Poe; The Lauson tragedy, by J. W. De Forest; The iron shroud, by W. Mudford; The bell tower, by H. Melville; The Kathayan slave, by E. C. Judson; The story of La Roche, by H. Mackenzie; The vision of sudden death, by T. De Quincey.

Same. Vol. IV. Life. Sq. 16°. Boston, 1875. 13 . 890

Contents. — Vol. IV. Rab and his friends, by John Brown, M.D.; A romance of real life, by W. D. Howells; The luck of Roaring camp, by Bret Harte; Jerry Jarvis's wig, by R. H. Barham; Beauty and the beast, by N. P. Willis; David Swan, by N. Hawthorne; Dreamthorp, by A. Smith; A bachelor's revery, by D. G. Mitchell; The grammar of life, by B. F. Taylor; My chateaux, by G. W. Curtis; Dream children, by C. Lamb; The man in the reservoir, by C. F. Hoffman; Westminster Abbey, by J. Addison; The Puritans, by T. B. Macaulay; Gettysburg, by A. Lincoln.

JOHNSON, *Dr.* Samuel. Life and conversations of. Alexander Main. 8°. London, 1874 . . . . 13 . 1253
JOHNSON, S. J. Eclipses, past and future; with general hints for observing the heavens. Sm. 8°. Oxford and London, 1874 . . . . 13 . 859
JONES, John Paul, Life of. J. S. C. Abbott. 12°. New York, 1874 . . 13 . 109
JONES, Thomas Rymer. Mammalia: a popular introduction to natural history. With 200 illustrations. Sm. 8°. London [n. d.] . . . . 13 . 116
The natural history of birds: a popular introduction to ornithology. With 225 illustrations. Sm. 8°. London, 1872 . . . . 13 . 117

JONVEAUX, Emile. Two years in East Africa: adventures in Abyssinia and Nubia, with a journey to the sources of the Nile. Maps and numerous illustrations. Sm. 8°. London, 1875 . . . . 13 . 965
JOSEPH in the snow. B. Auerbach. 16°. New York, 1874 . . . . . . 4 . 855
JOSEPH Noirel's revenge. V. Cherbuliez. 16°. New York, 1872 . . . 4 . 858
JOSEPH Wilmot. G. W. M. Reynolds. 8°. Philadelphia [n. d.] . . . 4 . 532
JOURNAL of the Franklin institute. Vols. 67 and 68. 8°. Philadelphia, 1874 . . . . 17 . 463–64
JOURNAL of the reigns of King George IV., and King William IV., by the late C. C. F. Greville. Edited by Henry Reeve. 3 v. 8°. London. 1874 . . . . 13 . 1050–52
JOURNEY from the Indus to the Tigris in 1872. Henry Walter Bellew. L. 8°. London, 1874 . . . . 13 . 1329
JOURNEY (A) to the centre of the earth. Jules Verne. Sq. 16°. Boston [n. d.] . . . . 4 . 1227
JOURNEY (A) to the north pole. Jules Verne. Sm. 8°. New York, 1875. 2 copies . . . . 4 . 1228–29
JUDICIAL dramas; or, the romance of French criminal law. Henry Spicer. 8°. London, 1872 . . . . 13 . 1218
JULIUS; or, the street boy out west. H. Alger, jun. 16°. Boston, 1874. 2 copies . . . . 4 . 1165–66
JUNE, Jennie [*Pseud.*]. *See* CROLY, Jennie C.
JUPITER's daughters. C. Jenkin. 16°. New York, 1874 . . . . 4 . 868
JUSTIN Harley. J. E. Cooke. 12°. Philadelphia, 1874 . . . . 4 . 458

K.

*KAMES (Henry Home), *Lord.* Art of thinking. 12°. New York, 1818 . 13 . 865
*Essays on the principles of morality and natural religion. 8°. Edinburgh, 1779 . . . . 13 . 1207
KATHERINE Earle. A. Trafton. Sm. 7°. Boston, 1875 . . . . 4 . 354
KEBLE, *Rev.* John. Memoir of. *Sir* J. T. Coleridge. Sm. 8°. London, 1874. . . . . 13 . 158
KEEL and saddle. J. W. Revere. 12°. Boston, 1873 . . . . 13 . 1155
KELLOGG, Elijah. *Elm Island series.* 6 v. 16°. Boston, 1875. Illustrated.
Lion Ben of Elm Island . . . . 4 . 940
Charlie Bell, the waif of Elm Island . . . . 4 . 941
The ark of Elm Island . . . . 4 . 942
The boy farmers of Elm Island . . . . 4 . 943
The young ship-builders of Elm Island . . . . 4 . 944
The hard-scrabble of Elm Island . . . . 4 . 945

Forest Glen series. 1 v. 16°. Boston, 1875. Illustrated.
Sowed by the wind; or, the poor boy's fortune . . . . 4 . 946

Pleasant Cove series. 6 v. 16°. Boston, 1874. Illustrated.
Arthur Brown, the young captain . . . . 4 . 947
The young deliverers of Pleasant Cove . . . . 4 . 948
The cruise of the Casco . . . . 4 . 949

KELLOGG, Elijah. *Pleasant Cove Series (continued).*
The child of the island glen . . . . 4 . 950
John Godsoe's legacy . . . . 4 . 951
The fisher boys of Pleasant Cove . . . . 4 . 952

Whispering Pine series. 6 v. 16°. Boston, 1875. Illustrated.
The spark of genius; or, the college life of James Trafton . . . . . . 4 . 953
The sophomores of Radcliffe; or, James Trafton and his bosom friends . 4 . 954
The whispering pine; or, the graduates of Radcliffe Hall . . . . 4 . 955
Winning his spurs; or, Henry Morton's first trial . . . . 4 . 956
The turning of the tide; or, Radcliffe Rich and his patients . . . . . 4 . 957
A stout heart; or, the student from over the sea . . . . 4 . 958
KENILWORTH. *Sir* W. Scott. 2 v. in 1. 12°. Boston, 1874 . . . . 4 . 224
KENNETH. G. W. M. Reynolds. 8°. Philadelphia [n. d.] . . . . . . 4 . 534
KIDD, Captain William. J. S. C. Abbott. 12°. New York, 1874 . . . 13 . 110
KING, *Rev.* Charles William. The hand-book of engraved gems. With numerous illustrations. 8°. London, 1866 . . . . 13 . 1254
The natural history of gems; or, decorative stones. 8°. London, 1867. 13 . 1255
KING'S (The) own. F. Marryat. 12°. London, 1873 . . . . 4 . 241
KINGSLEY, *Rev.* Charles. Health and education. 12°. New York, 1874. 13 . 101
The heroes; or, Greek fairy tales for my children. Illustrations. Sm. 8°. London, 1873 . . . . 4 . 459
Plays and Puritans, and other historical essays. 1 plate. Sm. 8°. London, 1873 . . . . 13 . 102
Prose idyls, new and old. Sm. 8°. London, 1872 . . . . 13 . 103
The water-babies; a fairy tale for a land baby. Illustrations. Sm. 8°. London, 1872 . . . . 4 . 460
KINGSLEY, Henry. Tales of old travel re-narrated. Illustrated. Sm. 8°. London, 1870 . . . . 4 . 465
KINGSTON, William H. G. Charley Laurel: a story of adventure by sea and land. Illustrated. Sm. 8°. London [n. d.]. 2 copies . . . 4 . 929–30
In the wilds of Africa. A tale for boys. Illustrated. 8°. London, 1872 4 . 931
The pirate's treasure, a legend of Panama; and other amusing tales for boys, and for soldiers and sailors on land and sea. 16°. New York 1869. . . . . 4 . 932
Stories of animal sagacity. 60 illustrations. Sm. 8°. London, 1874. 4 . 933
KITCHIN, G. W. A history of France down to the year 1453. Sm. 8°. Oxford, 1873 . . . . 13 . 150
KNATCHBULL-HUGESSEN, E. H. Whispers from fairy-land. Illustrated. Sm. 8°. New York, 1875 . . . . 4 . 365
KNIGHT (The) of Gwynne. C. Lever. Sm. 8°. London, 1873 . . . . 4 . 413
KNIGHTLY (The) heart, and other poems. J. F. Colman. 16°. Boston, 1873. 21 . 230
KNOX, John, and his times. *Miss* Warren. 16°. New York [n. d.] . . 13 . 969
KOHLRAUSCH, Frederick. A history of Germany from the earliest period to the present time. Trans. from the last German edition by James D. Haas. 8°. New York, 1873 . . . . 13 . 1313
*KOLBEN, Peter. The present state of the Cape of Good Hope; or, a particular account of the several nations of the Hottentots, with a short account of the Dutch settlement at the Cape. Done into English from the original by Mr. Medley. Illustrated with copper plates. 8°. London, 1731 . . . . 13 . 913

L.

*LACROIX, Paul. [*Bibliophile Jacob*] Manners, customs, and dress during the middle ages, and during the renaissance period. 15 chromolithographic prints by Kellerhoven, and upwards of 400 engravings on wood. 4°. New York, 1874 . . . . 13 . 1528

*Military and religious life in the middle ages and at the period of the renaissance. 14 chromolithographic prints by Kellerhoven, Régamey, and Allard, and upwards of 400 engravings on wood. 4°. New York, 1874, ... 13 . 1529

LADY (The) of the isle. E. D. E. N. Southworth. 12°. Philadelphia, 1859. 4 . 1025

LADY (The) of Lawford. N. B. Warren. 12°. Troy, 1874 . . . . . . 4 . 561

*LAKE and mountain scenery of the Swiss Alps, by G. Closs and O. Froelicher; with text by T. G. Bonney. Roy. 4°. New York and Boston [n. d.] . . . . 15 . 1414

LAMB, Mary and Charles. Poems, letters, and remains: now first collected, with reminiscences and notes, by W. Carew Hazlitt. With portrait, and numerous fac-similes and illustrations of their favorite haunts in London and the suburbs. Sm. 8°. London, 1874 . . . 13 . 118

LANCASHIRE (The) witches. W. H. Ainsworth. 16°. London [n. d.] . 4 . 1173

LAND (The) of the Forum and Vatican. Newman Hall. 16°. New York [n.d.] 13 . 1178

LAND (The) of the white elephant. F. Vincent, jun. 8°. New York, 1874 . 13 . 1340

LARCOM, Lucy. Childhood songs. Illustrated. Sq. 8°. Boston, 1875 . 21 . 226

LAST journals of David Livingstone in Central Africa. H. Waller. L. 8°. New York, 1875 . . . . 13 . 1310

LAST (The) of the Mohicans. J. F. Cooper. 12°. New York, 1875 . . 4 . 1052

LAUDER, *Sir* Thomas Dick. Scottish rivers. With illustrations by the author. Preface by John Brown. Sm. 8°. Edinburgh, 1874 . . 13 . 147

LAUGEL, Auguste. England political and social. Trans. by James Morgan Hart. 16°. New York, 1874 . . . . 13 . 949

LAZARUS, Emma. Alide: an episode of Goethe's life. 12°. Philadelphia, 1874 . . . . 4 . 478

LEARNED societies and printing clubs. *Rev.* A. Hume. Sm. 8°. London, 1853. 13 . 151

LE BRETON, Anna Letitia, *editor.* Correspondence of William Ellery Channing, D.D., and Lucy Aikin, from 1826 to 1842. Sm. 8°. Boston, 1874 . . . . 13 . 838

LECTURES on the history of ancient philosophy. William Archer Butler. Edited from the author's MSS., with notes by William Hepworth Thompson. 8°. London, 1874 . . . . 13 . 1419

LECTURES (Two) on sacred poetry of early religions. R. W. Church. Sm. 8°. London, 1874 . . . . 21 . 252

LEE, Holme [*Pseud.*]. *See* PARR, Harriet.

LEE, Samuel. The Bible regained, and the God of the Bible ours: or, the system of religious truth in outline. 16°. Boston, 1874 . . . . 13 . 861

LEECH (The) club. G. W. Owen. 12°. Boston, 1874 . . . . 4 . 260

LEGENDS of Saint Patrick. Aubrey De Vere. Sm. 8°. London, 1872 . 21 . 237

LEICESTER square; its associations and worthies. Tom Taylor. Sm. 2°. London, 1874 . . . . 13 . 947

LEISURE hour series. 16°. *Namely:—*

Alcestis. New York, 1874 . . . . 4 . 952

LEISURE hour series (*continued*).
Alexander, *Mrs.* Which shall it be? New York, 1874 . . . . . . 4 . 853
The wooing o't. New York, 1873 . . . . 4 . 854
Auerbach, B. Joseph in the snow. New York, 1874 . . . . . . 4 . 855
Auerbach, B. The little barefoot. New York, 1874 . . . . 4 . 856
Calverley, C. S. Fly leaves. New York, 1872 . . . . 21 . 249
Cherbuliez, V. Count Kostia. New York, 1873 . . . . 4 . 857
Joseph Noirel's revenge. New York, 1872 . . . . 4 . 858
Prosper. New York, 1874 . . . . 4 . 859
Craven, P. Fleurange. New York, 1873 . . . . 4 . 860
Droz, G. Around a spring. New York, 1873 . . . . 4 . 861
Babolain. New York, 1873 . . . . 4 . 862
Freytag, G. Ingraban. New York, 1873 . . . . 4 . 863
Hardy, T. Desperate remedies. New York, 1874 . . . . 4 . 864
Far from the madding crowd. New York, 1874 . . . . 4 . 865
Under the greenwood tree. New York, 1874 . . . . 4 . 866
Heine, H. Scintillations. New York, 1873 . . . . 4 . 867
Jenkin, *Mrs.* C. Jupiter's daughters. New York, 1874 . . . . . . 4 . 868
"Who breaks — pays." New York, 1873 . . . . 4 . 869
Parr, L. Hero Carthew. New York, 1873 . . . . 4 . 870
Turgenieff, J. S. Liza. New York, 1873 . . . . 4 . 871
On the eve. New York, 1873 . . . . 4 . 872
Spring floods: and, A lear of the steppe. New York, 1874 . . . 4 . 873
LENA Rivers. M. J. Holmes. 12°. New York, 1874. 2 copies . . . 3 . 1353–54
LENZEN, Marie. Not in their set; or, in different circles of society. A novel. Trans. from the German by M. S. 12°. Boston, 1874 . . 4 . 1140
LESTER, A. Hoyle. The Pre-Adamite; or, who tempted Eve? Scripture and science in unison, as respects the antiquity of man. 16°. Philadelphia, 1875 . . . . 13 . 1159
LESTER, C. Edwards. Life and public services of Charles Sumner. Portrait. L. 8°. New York, 1874 . . . . 13 . 1314
LEVER, Charles James. The adventures of Arthur O'Leary. Sm. 8°. London [n. d.] . . . . 4 . 401
Barrington. Sm. 8°. London [n. d.] . . . . 4 . 402
The Bramleighs of Bishop's folly. Sm. 8°. London, 1873 . . . . 4 . 403
Charles O'Malley, the Irish dragoon. Sm. 8°. London, 1872 . . . 4 . 404
The confessions of Con Cregan, the Irish Gil Blas. Sm. 8°. London [n. d.] . . . . 4 . 405
The Daltons; or, three roads in life. Sm. 8°. London, 1872 . . . 4 . 406
Davenport Dunn: a man of our day. Sm. 8°. London, 1872 . . . 4 . 407
A day's ride: a life's romance. Sm. 8°. London [n. d.] . . . . . 4 . 408
The Dodd family abroad. Sm. 8°. London, 1872 . . . . 4 . 409
The fortunes of Glencore. Sm. 8°. London, 1873 . . . . 4 . 410
Harry Lorrequer. Sm. 8°. London, 1873 . . . . 4 . 411
Jack Hinton. Sm. 8°. London [n. d.] . . . . 4 . 412
The knight of Gwynne: a tale of the time of the union. Sm. 8°. London, 1873 . . . . 4 . 413
Lord Kilgobbin, a tale of Ireland in our own time. Sm. 8°. London, 1873. 4 . 414
Luttrell of Arran. Sm. 8°. London [n. d.] . . . . 4 . 415
The Martins of Cro' Martin. Sm. 8°. London, 1872 . . . . 4 . 416

LEVER, Charles James (*continued*).
Maurice Tiernay, the soldier of fortune. Sm. 8°. London [n. d.] . . 4 . 417
The O'Donoghue: a tale of Ireland fifty years ago. Sm. 8°. London, 1872 . . . . 4 . 418
One of them. Sm. 8°. London, 1873 . . . . 4 . 419
A rent in a cloud, and St. Patrick's eve. Sm. 8°. London [n. d.] . . 4 . 420
Roland Cashel. Sm. 8°. London, 1872 . . . . 4 . 421
Sir Brook Fosbrooke. Sm. 8°. London, 1873 . . . . 4 . 422
Sir Jasper Carew: his life and experiences. Sm. 8°. London, 1873 . 4 . 423
That boy of Norcott's. Sm. 8°. London, 1873 . . . . 4 . 424
Tom Burke of "ours." Sm. 8°. London, 1872 . . . . 4 . 425

LEWALD, Fanny. Hulda; or, the deliverer. A romance. Trans. from the German by *Mrs.* A. L. Wister. 12°. Philadelphia, 1874. 2 copies. 3 . 1367–8

Note. — The author was married to Adolf Stahr in 1855, but she continues to publish under her maiden name.

LEWES, George Henry. Problems of life and mind. First series. The foundations of a creed. Vol. 1. 8°. Boston, 1874 . . . . . 13 . 1256

LEWIS, Charlton T. A history of Germany from the earliest times. Founded on *Dr.* David Müller's "History of the German people." 8°. New York, 1874 . . . . 13 . 1139

LEWIS, David, *translator.* The book of the foundations of St. Teresa of Jesus, of the order of our Lady of Carmel, written by herself. 8°. London, 1871 . . . . 13 . 1067

LEWIS, Dio. Five-minute chats with young women, and certain other parties. Sm. 8°. New York, 1874 . . . . 13 . 948

LEWIS, Richard. History of the life-boat, and its work. Illustrations. Sm. 8°. London, 1874 . . . . 13 . 1146

LEYDEN, John. Poetical remains, with memoirs of his life, by *Rev.* James Morton. 8°. London, 1819 . . . . 21 . 210

LIBRARY of fathers of the Holy Catholic Church. Historical tracts of St. Athanasius, archbishop of Alexandria. Trans. with notes and indices. 8°. Oxford, 1843 . . . . 13 . 1324
Select treatises of St. Athanasius, archbishop of Alexandria, in controversy with the Arians. Trans. with notes and indices. 8°. Oxford, 1842 . . . . 13 . 1325

LIBRARY (The) of foreign romance: comprising original translations from the most celebrated continental authors. Edited by J. C. James, Esq. 9 v. 8°. London, 1846–7.

Vol. I. Dumas, A. The three musketeers. Trans. from the French by W. Barrow . . . . 4 . 440
II. Hauff, Wilhelm. Lichtenstein; or, the Swabian league. Trans. from the German by F. Woodley and W. Lander . . . . 4 . 441
III. Dumas, A. Twenty years after. Sequel to "The three musketeers." Trans. from the French by W. Barrow. Vol. I. . . . 4 . 442
IV. Twenty years after. Vol. II. . . . . 4 . 443
V. Godway Castle; or, the fortunes of a king's daughter. Edited from the papers of the Duchess of Nottingham, by Mme. Palzow. Trans. from the German by F. K. Barnard . . . . . 4 . 444
VI. Dumas, A. Isabel of Bavaria; or, the chronicles of France for the reign of Charles VI. Trans. from the French by W. Barrow . . . . 4 . 445
VII. Ingemann, B. S. The childhood of King Erik Menved. Trans. from the Danish by J. Kesson . . . . 4 . 446

VIII. Van Lennep, J. The Rose of Dekama. Trans. from the Dutch by F. Woodley . . . . 4 . 447
IX. Lavergne, A. de. The secret of the confessional. A legend of Aubergne. The last lord of the manor, and The count of Mansfeldt. Trans. from the French by Milicent Hack . . . . . 4 . 448

LIEBIG, Justus. Chemistry in its applications to agriculture and physiology. Edited from the MSS. of the author, by Lyon Playfair and William Gregory. 12°. New York, 1847 . . . . 13 . 847
LIFE and conversations of *Dr.* Samuel Johnson. Alexander Main. 8°. London, 1874 . . . . 13 . 1253
LIFE and death of John of Barneveld. John L. Motley. 2 v. 8°. New York, 1874 . . . . 13 . 1412–13
*LIFE (The) and habits of wild animals. Illustrated from designs by Joseph Wolf, with descriptive letter-press by Daniel Giraud Elliot. 4°. New York, 1874 . . . . 13 . 1501
LIFE and labors of Thomas Brassey. *Sir* Arthur Helps. 8°. Boston, 1874. 13 . 1355
LIFE and literature in the fatherland. J. F. Hurst. 8°. New York, 1875. 13 . 1136
LIFE and public services of Charles Sumner. C. E. Lester. L. 8°. New York, 1874 . . . . 13 . 1314
LIFE and wanderings in Eastern Africa. Charles New. Sm. 8°. London, 1874 . . . . 13 . 132
LIFE in Danbury. J. M. Bailey. Sq. 8°. Boston, 1873 . . . . 4 . 822
LIFE in the East Indies. W. H. Thomes. 12°. Boston, 1875 . . . . 4 . 1134
LIFE (The) of Christ. Frederic W. Farrar. 2 v. 8°. New York, 1874. 13 . 1342–43
LIFE of Thomas, first Lord Denman. *Sir* Joseph Arnould. 2 v. 8°. Boston, 1874 . . . . 13 . 1331–32
LIFE of Charles Dickens. J. Forster. Vol. 3. 12°. Philadelphia, 1874 . 13 . 162
LIFE of Admiral A. H. Foote, U. S. N. J. M. Hoppin. 8°. New York, 1874 . . . . 13 . 1350
LIFE of Edwin Forrest. James Rees. 12°. Philadelphia, 1874 . . . . 13 . 133
LIFE of Benjamin Franklin, from his own writings. Edited by John Bigelow. 3 v. 12°. Philadelphia, 1874 . . . . 13 . 344–46
LIFE of *Gen.* H. Havelock. J. T. Headley. 12°. New York, 1854 . . 13 . 951
LIFE of Thomas Jefferson. J. Parton. 8°. Boston, 1874 . . . . . . 13 . 1249
LIFE of John Paul Jones. J. S. C. Abbott. 12°. New York, 1874 . . 13 . 109
*LIFE of Sethos. John Terrasson. 2 v. 8°. London, 1732 . . . . 13 . 841–42
LIFE (The) of John Sterling. T. Carlyle. 16°. New York, 1871 . . . 13 . 867
LIFE (The) of a sailor. W. James. 12°. London [n. d.] . . . . . . 4 . 436
LIFE without and life within. S. M. F. Ossoli. 12°. Boston, 1874 . . . 13 . 128
LIGHTNING express. W. T. Adams. 16°. Boston, 1875 . . . . . . 4 . 315
LILY (A) among thorns. Emma Marshall. 16°. New York, 1874 . . . 4 . 477
LILY (The) and the cross. J. De Mille. 16°. Boston, 1875 2 copies 4 . 913–14
LINCOLN and Seward. Gideon Welles. 16°. New York, 1874 . . . . 13 . 163
LINDSAY, W. S. History of merchant shipping and ancient commerce. Vols. 1, 2. With numerous illustrations. 2 v. 8°. Lond., 1874. 13 . 1335–36
LINLEY Rochford. J. McCarthy. 8°. New York, 1874 . . . . 4 . 521
LINTON, Eliza Lynn. Patricia Kemball. A novel. 12°. Philadelphia, 1875. 2 copies . . . . 4 . 923–24
LION Ben of Elm Island. E. Kellogg. 16°. Boston, 1875 . . . . . . 4 . 940
LIONEL Lincoln. J. F. Cooper. 12°. New York, 1873 . . . . 4 . 1053
LITERARY remains of the late Emanuel Deutsch, with a brief memoir. 8°. New York, 1874 . . . . 13 . 1230

LITTELL'S living age. Vols. 117 to 123 inclusive. 8°. Boston, 1873–74 . 12 . 1–7
LITTLE (The) Barefoot. B. Auerbach. 16°. New York, 1874 . . . . 4 . 856
LITTLE Bobtail. W. T. Adams. 16°. Boston, 1875 . . . . 4 . 338
LITTLE by little. W. T. Adams. 16°. Boston, 1875 . . . . 4 . 313
LITTLE classics. *See* JOHNSON, Rossiter.
LITTLE Dorrit. C. Dickens. 2 v. 12°. Boston, 1875 . . . . 4 . 1315–16
LITTLE (The) lame prince. D. M. Craik. Sq. 16°. New York, 1875 . . 4 . 454
LITTLE people of God. Ed. by *Mrs.* G. L. Austin. 16°. Boston, 1874 . 21 . 229
LITTLE wide-awake. Lucy D. S. Barker. Sm. 4°. London and New York, 1875 . . . . 4 . 554
LIVE lights or dead lights. (Altar or table?) Hargrave Jennings. Sm. 8°. London, 1873 . . . . 13 . 115
LIVES, character, speeches, and statesmanship of John Wilkes, Richard Brinsley Sheridan, and Charles James Fox, the opposition under George the Third. W. F. Rae. 12°. New York, 1874 . . . . 13 . 935
LIVINGSTONE, David. Last journals of, in Central Africa. H. Waller. L. 8°. New York, 1875 . . . . 13 . 1310
LIZA; or, "a nest of nobles." Ivan S. Turgénieff. 16°. New York, 1873. 4 . 871
LLOYD, Dalan. Mary Densel. 16°. New York, 1874 . . . . 4 . 879
LLOYD, H. A. [*Old Shekarry.*] The forest and the field. 8 illustrations. Sm. 8°. London, 1874 . . . . 4 . 475
Wrinkles; or, hints to sportsmen and travellers, on dress, equipment, and camp-life. Illustrated. Sm. 8°. London, 1874 . . . . 4 . 476
LOCKER, Arthur [*Pseud.*]. *See* FORBES, J. H.
LONDON characters. H. Mayhew. 8°. London, 1874 . . . . 13 . 1162
LONG, Joseph W. American wild-fowl shooting; describing the haunts, habits, and methods of shooting wild fowl, particularly those of the western States of America. With instruction concerning guns, blinds, &c. 16°. New York, 1874 . . . . 13 . 1150
LORD, Willis. Christian theology for the people. 8°. New York, 1875 . 13 . 1316
LORD Kilgobbin. C. Lever. Sm. 8°. London, 1873 . . . . 4 . 414
LORD Saxondale. G. W. M. Reynolds. 8°. Philadelphia [n. d.] . . . 4 . 535
LORD of himself. F. H. Underwood. 12°. Boston, 1874 . . . . 4 . 934
LORIMER, George C. Under the evergreens; or, a night with St. Nicholas. Illustrated. Sq. 16°. Boston, 1874 . . . . 4 . 834
LOSING to win. T. Davies. 12°. New York, 1874 . . . . 4 . 266
LOSS and gain. John H. Newman. Sm. 8°. London, 1874 . . . . . . 13 . 923
LOST forever. L. T. Townsend. 16°. Boston, 1875 . . . . 4 . 369
LOST (The) heir of Linlithgow. E. D. E. N. Southworth. 12°. Philadelphia, 1872 . . . . 4 . 1026
LOST (The) heiress. E. D. E. N. Southworth. 12°. Philadelphia, 1854 . 4 . 1028
LOST Lenore. M. Reid. 12°. New York, 1874 . . . . 4 . 1248
LOST (The) model. H. Hooper. 12°. Philadelphia, 1874 . . . . 4 . 254
LOUDON, Jane Webb. The mummy! A tale of the twenty-second century. 16°. London [n. d.] . . . . 4 . 846
LOVE ("L'amour"). Trans. from the French of Jules Michelet, by J. W. Palmer. 12°. New York, 1874 . . . . 4 . 1139
LOVE (The) match. H. Cockton. Sm. 8°. London [n. d.] . . . . . . 4 . 577
"LOVE me little, love me long." C. Reade. Sm. 8°. Boston, 1875 . . 4 . 1123
LOVE'S labor won. E. D. E. N. Southworth. 12°. Philadelphia, 1862 . 4 . 1029

LOWELL, Robert Traill Spence. Anthony Brade. (Fiction.) 16°. Boston, 1874. 2 copies . . . . 4 . 927–28

LÖWIG, Carl. Principles of organic and physiological chemistry. Trans. by Daniel Breed, M. D. 8°. Philadelphia, 1853. . . . . 13 . 1405

LUARD, Julia. Clare Savile; or, sixty years ago. Illustrations. Sm. 8°. London [n. d.] . . . . 4 . 806

LUCK and pluck. H. Alger, jun. 16°. Boston, 1869 . . . . 4 . 1147

LUCK is every thing. W. H. Maxwell. Sm. 8°. London [n. d.] . . . 4 . 431

LUCY Maria. A. M. Diaz. 16°. Boston, 1874 . . . . 4 . 935

LUTTRELL of Arran. C. Lever. Sm. 8°. London [n. d.] . . . . 4 . 415

LYELL, *Sir* Charles. Principles of geology; or, the modern changes of the earth and its inhabitants, considered as illustrative of geology. Illustrated with maps, plates, and woodcuts. Vol. 2. 8°. New York, 1874 . 13 . 1053

> *Note.*—The first volume of *Sir* Charles Lyell's "Principles of Geology" will be found in Vol. 1 of the Catalogue. [No. 16. 1160.]

LYTTON, *Lord.* *See* BULWER-LYTTON, Edward (George Earle) Lytton, *Lord Lytton.*

LYTTON, (Edward) Robert. *See* BULWER-LYTTON, (Edward) Robert.

M.

M'CAUSLAND, Dominick. The builders of Babel. Sm. 8°. London, 1874. 13 . 1151

MCCARTHY, Justin. Linley Rochford. A novel. 8°. New York, 1874 . 4 . 521

MCCOSH, James. The Scottish philosophy, biographical, expository, critical, from Hutcheson to Hamilton. 8°. New York, 1875 . . . . 13 . 1422

MACEUEN, Malcolm. Celebrities of the past and present, chiefly adapted from Charles Augustin Sainte-Beuve. Sm. 8°. Philadelphia, 1874. 13 . 1268

> *Contents.*—Cardinal Richelieu; Cardinal Mazarin; Cardinal de Retz; Father Lacordaire; Montesquieu; Madame Récamier; Saint Evremond, and Ninon de l'Enclos; Lord Chesterfield; Adrienne Le Couvreur; Milton and poetry; Thackeray; Epilogue on Lord Lytton; The young captive, by André Chénier; Brother Eugenius, adapted from an old German legend.

MACGAHAN, J. A. Campaigning on the Oxus, and the fall of Khiva. With map and illustrations. 8°. New York, 1874 . . . . 13 . 1353

MACKENZIE, Adelheid Shelton. Aureola; or, the black sheep. A story of German social life. 16°. Philadelphia, 1871 . . . . 4 . 364

MACLEOD, Norman. The starling. Illustrated. 16°. New York [n. d.] 4 . 1137

*MACLISE, Daniel. A gallery of illustrious literary characters (1830–1838). Accompanied by notices, chiefly by the late William Maginn. Edited by William Bates, with a preface and copious notes, biographical, critical, bibliographical, and generally illustrative. 84 plates. 4°. London [n. d.] . . . . 13 . 1514

MACMICHAEL, W. F. The Oxford and Cambridge boat races. A chronicle of the contests on the Thames, in which university crews have borne a part, from A.D. 1829 to A. D. 1869. Compiled from the university club books, and other contemporary and authentic records; with maps of the racing courses, index of names, and an introduction on rowing, and its value as an art and recreation. Sm. 8°. Cambridge, 1870 . . . . 13 . 876

McPherson, Edward. Hand-book of politics for 1874; being a record of important political action, national and State, from July 15, 1872, to July 15, 1874. 8°. Washington, 1874 . . . . 13 . 1411
Macquoid, Katherine S. A charming widow; or, wild as a hawk. 12°. New York, 1874 . . . . 4 . 366
*Madox, Thomas. Formulare Anglicanum; or, a collection of ancient charters and instruments of divers kinds, taken from the originals, placed under several heads, and deduced (in a series according to the order of time) from the Norman conquest, to the end of the reign of King Henry VIII. Folio. London, 1702 . . . . 13 . 1505
*Maetzner, Edward. An English grammar: methodical, analytical, and historical. With a treatise on the orthography, prosody, inflections, and syntax of the English tongue; and numerous authorities cited in order of historical development. Trans. from the German with the sanction of the author, by Clair James Grece. 3 v. 8°. London and Boston, 1874 . . . . 13 . 1551–53

Note. — This work is the most comprehensive treatise on the English language that has yet appeared.

Maiden (The) of Treppi. P. Heyse. 16°. New York, 1874 . . . . . . 4 . 830
Maiden (The) widow. E. D. E. N. Southworth. 12°. Philadelphia, 1870. 4 . 1019
Main, Alexander. Life and conversations of Dr. Samuel Johnson (founded chiefly upon Boswell). With a preface by George Henry Lewes. 8°. London, 1874 . . . . 13 . 1253
Make or break. W. T. Adams. 16°. Boston, 1875 . . . . 4 . 324
Mammalia. T. R. Jones. Sm. 8°. London [n. d.] . . . . 13 . 116
Man (A) in earnest. R. Collyer. 16°. Boston, 1875 . . . . 13 . 864
Man (The) of many friends. T. Hook. 16°. London [n. d.] . . . . . 4 . 815
Man on the ocean. R. M. Ballantyne. Sm. 8°. London, 1874 . . . . 4 . 1205
Man's immortality, The mode of. *Rev.* T. A. Goodwin. 12°. New York, 1874 . . . . 13 . 145
*Manners, customs, and dress during the middle ages, and at the period of the renaissance. Paul Lacroix. 4°. New York, 1874 . . . . . . 13 . 1528
Manual of mythology. A. S. Murray. Sm. 8°. London, 1873. . . . 13 . 1169
*Marcoy, Paul. Travels in South America from the Pacific ocean to the Atlantic ocean. Trans. from the French by Elihu Rich. Illustrated by 525 engravings on wood, drawn by E. Riou, and 10 maps from drawings by the author. 2 v. 4°. New York, 1875 . . . . . 13 . 1507–8
Marey, E. J. Animal mechanism: a treatise on terrestrial and aërial locomotion. 117 illustrations. Sm. 8°. New York, 1874 . . . . . . 13 . 1143
Maria Monk's daughter; an autobiography. *Mrs.* L. St. John Eckel. 8°. New York, 1874 . . . . 4 . 548
Marian Grey. M. J. Holmes. 12°. New York, 1874. 2 copies . . 3 . 1355–56
Mariner's (The) chronicle of shipwrecks, fires, famines, and other disasters at sea. Sixty engravings. 2 v. in 1. 12°. Philadelphia, 1849 . . . . 13 . 950
Marion Berkley. L. B. Comins. 16°. Boston, 1870 . . . . 4 . 464
Marjorie's quest. Jeanie T. Gould. 16°. Boston, 1875 . . . . 4 . 559
Mark Gildersleeve. J. S. Sauzade. 12°. New York, 1873 . . . . . . 4 . 1138
Mark the match-boy. H. Alger, jun. 16°. Boston, 1869. . . . . . . 4 . 1157

Marks and monograms on pottery and porcelain. Collector's hand-book. W. Chaffers. Sm. 8°. London, 1874 . . . . 13 . 856
Marlitt, E. [*Pseud.*]. *See* John, Eugenie.
Maroon (The). M. Reid. 12°. New York, 1874 . . . . 4 . 1249
Marriage. M. Ferrier. 16°. London [n. d.]. . . . . 4 . 826
Marryat, *Capt.* Frederick. The dog fiend; or, Snarleyyow. Illustrations. 12°. London, 1873 . . . . 4 . 237
Frank Mildmay; or, the naval officer. With a memoir of Capt. Marryat by Florence Marryat. Illustrated. 12. London [n. d.] . 4 . 238
Jacob Faithful. Illustrated. 12°. London, 1873. . . . . 4 . 239
Japhet in search of a father. Illustrations. 12°. London, 1873 . . 4 . 240
The King's own. Illustrated. 12°. London, 1873 . . . . 4 . 241
Mr. Midshipman Easy. Illustrated. 12°. London, 1873 . . . . . 4 . 242
Newton Foster; or, the merchant service. Illustrated. 12°. London, 1873 . . . . 4 . 243
The Pacha of many tales. Illustrated. 12°. London, 1873 . . . 4 . 244
Percival Keene. Illustrated. 12°. London [n. d.] . . . . 4 . 245
Peter Simple. Portrait of author, and illustrations. 12°. London, 1873 . . . . 4 . 246
The phantom ship. Illustrated. 12°. London, 1874 . . . . 4 . 247
The poacher. Illustrated. 12°. London [n. d.] . . . . 4 . 248
Olla podrida. Illustrated. 12°. London, 1874 . . . . 4 . 249
editor. Rattlin the reefer. Illustrated. 12°. London, 1873 . . . 4 . 250
The travels and adventures of Monsieur Violet in California, Sonora, and Western Texas. Illustrated. 12°. London, 1874 . . . . . 4 . 251
Valerie, an autobiography. Illustrated. 12°. London [n. d.] . . 4 . 252
Marsh, George Perkins. The earth as modified by human action. A new edition of Man and nature. 8°. New York, 1874 . . . . 13 . 1306

Note. — "In preparing for the press an Italian translation [of Man and nature], published at Florence in 1870, I made numerous corrections in the statements of both facts and opinions; I incorporated into the text, and introduced in notes, a large amount of new data and other illustrative matter. . . . In the present edition, which is based on the Italian translation, I have made many further corrections and changes of arrangement of the original matter; I have rewritten a considerable portion of the work, and have made, in the text and in notes, numerous and important additions." — *Preface.*

Marshall, Emma. Edward's wife. 16°. New York [n. d.] . . . . . 4 . 844
A lily among thorns. 16°. New York, 1874 . . . . 4 . 477
Martin Chuzzlewit. C. Dickens. 2 v. 12°. Boston, 1872 . . . . . 4 . 1317–18
Martins (The) of Cro' Martin. C. Lever. Sm. 8°. London, 1872 . . 4 . 416
Martyn, W. Carlos. The pilgrim fathers of New England: a history. 12°. New York, 1867 . . . . 13 . 171
*Martyrs of the revolution (1649). Illustrated by *Sir* Anthony Vandyke and others. (*See* Prints, King Charles I.) 4°. London, 1746 . . 13 . 1516
Mary Price. G. W. M. Reynolds. 8°. Philadelphia [n. d.] . . . . . 4 . 537
Mary Queen of Scots, and her accusers. John Hosack. 8°. Edinburgh and London, 1869 . . . . 13 . 1222
Massachusetts. Adjutant general's annual report for the years ending Dec. 31, 1865, 1866, 1867, and 1868. 8°. Boston, 1866–69 . 11 . 1246–49
Agriculture, Twenty-first annual report of the secretary of the board of, for 1873–74. 8°. Boston, 1874 . . . . 11 . 1031

MASSACHUSETTS (*continued*).
Charities, Tenth annual report of the board of state charities for 1872–73. 8°. Boston, 1874 . . . . 11 . 1118
Education. Annual reports of the board, 1871–73. 3 v. 8°. Boston, 1872–74 . . . . 11 . 814–16
Health. Annual report of the board of, for year ending January, 1874. 8°. Boston, 1874 . . . . 11 . 1142
Index of the special railroad laws of Massachusetts, 1826–73. Edward L. Pierce. 8°. Boston, 1874 . . . . 11 . 1250
Labor statistics, 1874. 8°. Boston, 1874 . . . . 11 . 905
Manual for the general court, for the years 1857–59–60–61–64–65–66–67–68–69–71–72–73–74–75. 15 v. 12°. Boston, 1857–75 . . . 11 . 832–46
Railroad commissioner's report for 1873. 8°. Boston, 1874 . . . . 11 . 939
Reports of controverted elections in the House of Representatives, from 1780 to 1852. Roy. 8°. Boston, 1853 . . . . 11 . 1251

MASSON, David. Chatterton: a story of the year 1770. Sm. 8°. London, 1874 . . . . 13 . 104

Note. — Reprinted from the author's Essays biographical and critical: chiefly on English poets, published in 1856, with corrections. — *Prefatory Note.*

Editor. The poetical works of John Milton, with introductions, notes, and an essay on Milton's English. Portrait. 3 v. 8°. London, 1874 . . . . 21 . 206–8
Wordsworth, Shelley, Keats, and other essays. Sm. 8°. London, 1874. 13 . 105

Contents. — Wordsworth; Scottish influence in British literature: Life and poetry of Shelley; Life and poetry of Keats; Theories of poetry; Prose and verse; De Quincey.

MATHEWS, Joanna H. Rosalie's pet. Illustrated. (Juvenile.) 16°. New York, 1875 . . . . 4 . 377

MATHEWS, William. The great conversers, and other essays. 8°. Chicago, 1874 . . . . 13 . 122

MAUDSLEY, Henry. Responsibility in mental disease. 12°. New York, 1874. 13 . 130

MAURICE Tiernay. C. Lever. Sm. 8°. London [n. d.] . . . . 4 . 417

MAXWELL. T. Hook. 16°. London [n. d.] . . . . 4 . 816

MAXWELL, William Hamilton. The adventures of Capt. Blake; or, my life. Sm. 8°. London [n. d.] . . . . 4 . 426
Adventures of Capt. O'Sullivan. Sm. 8°. London [n. d.] . . . . 4 . 427
The bivouac; or, stories of the Peninsular war. Sm. 8°. London [n. d.] . . . . 4 . 428
Flood and field; or, the recollections of a soldier of fortune. Sm. 8°. London [n. d.] . . . . 4 . 429
The fortunes of Hector O'Halloran. Sm. 8°. London [n. d.] . . . 4 . 430
Luck is every thing; or, the adventures of Brian O'Linn. Sm. 8°. London [n. d.] . . . . 4 . 431
Stories of the Peninsular war. Sm. 8°. London [n. d.] . . . . . 4 . 432
Stories of Waterloo. Sm. 8°. London [n. d.] . . . . 4 . 433

MAYHEW, Henry, and *others.* London characters. Illustrations of the humor, pathos, and peculiarities of London life. With illustrations. 8°. London, 1874 . . . . 13 . 1162

MAYNE, Leger D. [*Pseud.*]. What shall we do to-night? or, social amusements for evening parties. . Illustrated. 12°. New York, 1873 . . 13 . 114
MAYO, Isabella Fivy. [*Edward Garrett.*] By still waters; a story for quiet hours. Illustrated. Sm. 8°. New York, 1874 . . . . . . 4 . 269
MAYO, William Starbuck. The Berber; or, the mountaineer of the Atlas. A tale of Morocco. 16°. New York, 1873 . . . . 4 . 558
MEADOW brook. M. J. Holmes. 12°. New York, 1874. 2 copies . . 3 . 1357–58
MEDII ævi kalendarium; or, dates, charters, and customs of the middle ages. R. T. Hampson. 2 v. 8°. London, 1841 . . . . 13 . 1214–15
*MELVIL, *Sir* James of Halhill, The memoirs of. Published from the original MSS. by George Scott. 8°. Edinburgh, 1735 . . . . . 13 . 846
MEMOIR and correspondence of W. E. Channing. 3 v. 12°. Boston, 1848. 13 . 829–31
MEMOIR and letters of Sara Coleridge. Edited by her daughter. 8°. New York, 1874 . . . . 13 . 1236
MEMOIR of William Blake. W. M. Rossetti. 16°. Boston, 1875 . . . 21 . 248
MEMOIR of the *Rev.* John Keble. *Sir* J. T. Coleridge. Sm. 8°. London, 1874 . . . . 13 . 158
MEMOIR of Samuel Slater. G. S. White. 8°. Philadelphia, 1836 . . . 13 . 1408
MEMOIRS of John Quincy Adams. Ed. by Charles Francis Adams. 3 v. 8°. Philadelphia, 1874 . . . . 13 . 1302–4
MEMOIRS of Bartholomew fair. H. Morley. Sm. 8°. London [n. d.] . 13 . 1171
*MEMOIRS of several ladies of Great Britain. George Ballard. 4°. Oxford, 1752 . . . . 13 . 1547
*MEMOIRS upon the art of war. *Count* Maurice de Saxe. 4°. London, 1757 . . . . 13 . 1527
*MEMORIAL of Charles Sumner. 4°. Boston, 1874 . . . . 13 . 1530
MEMORIES: a story of German love. Trans. from the German by George P. Upton. Sq. 16°. Chicago, 1875 . . . . 4 . 849
MEMORIES of French palaces. A. E. Challice. 8°. London, 1871 . . . 13 . 1148
MEMORIES of many men and some women. M. B. Field. 12°. New York, 1874 . . . . 13 . 152
MENTAL disease, Responsibility in. H. Maudsley. 12°. New York, 1874. 13 . 130
MENTAL physiology, Principles of. W. B. Carpenter. 8°. New York, 1874. 13 . 1265
MENZEL, Wolfgang. History of Germany from the earliest period to the present time. Trans. from the fourth German edition, by *Mrs.* George Horrocks. Plates. 3 v. Sm. 8°. London, 1871 . . . 13 . 956–58
MERCEDES of Castile. J. F. Cooper. 12°. New York, 1873 . . . . . 4 . 1054
MERCHANT shipping and ancient commerce, History of. W. S. Lindsay. 2 v. 8°. London, 1874 . . . . 13 . 1335–36
MERTON. T. Hook. 16°. London [n. d.] . . . . 4 . 817
MERVYN Clitheroe. W. H. Ainsworth. 16°. London [n. d.] . . . . 4 . 1174
MERY, Joseph. Through thick and thin: or, "La guerre du Nizam." Trans. from the French, by O. Vibeur. 12°. New York, 1874 . . . . . 4 . 474
*METALLURGY. Phillips, J. Arthur. Elements of metallurgy. Roy. 8°. London, 1874 . . . . 13 . 1549
MICHELET, Jules. Love ("L'amour"). Trans. from the fourth Paris edition, by J. W. Palmer. 12°. New York, 1874 . . . . 4 . 1139
MIÇHIELS, Alfred. Secret history of the Austrian government, and of its systematic persecutions of Protestants. Compiled from official documents. 8°. London, 1859 . . . . 13 . 1264

MILES Wallingford. J. F. Cooper. 12°. New York, 1873 . . . . . . 4 . 1041
*MILITARY and religious life during the middle ages, and at the period of the renaissance. Paul Lacroix. 4°. New York, 1874 . . . . . . 13 . 1529
MILL, John Stuart. Autobiography. 8°. New York, 1874 . . . . . . 13 . 1245
Principles of political economy. 2 v. 8°. Boston, 1848 . . . . . . 13 . 1423–24
MILLBANK. M. J. Holmes. 12°. New York, 1874. 2 copies. . . . 3 . 1359–60
MILLER, Joaquin. Unwritten history: life amongst the Modocs. Illustrated. 8°. Hartford, 1874 . . . . 4 . 547
MILTON, John. Poetical works. Edited with introductions and notes, by David Masson. 3 v. 8°. London, 1874 . . . . 21 . 2^6–8
MIRIAM. E. D. E. N. Southworth. 12°. Philadelphia, 1874 . . . . . . 4 . 103.
MIRIAM. M. V. Terhune. 12°. New York, 1874 . . . . 4 . 1111
MIRIAM Montfort. C. A. Warfield. 12°. New York, 1873 . . . . . . 4 . 268
MIRROR (The) of truth, and other (juvenile) stories. E. Hamerton. 16°. Boston, 1875 . . . . 4 . 568
MISCELLANEOUS writings. B. Green. 12°. Whitesboro', 1841 . . . . 13 . 854
MISCHIEF's thanksgiving. (Juvenile.) S. C. Woolsey. 16°. Boston, 1874. 4 . 570
MISER's (The) daughter. W. H. Ainsworth. 16°. London [n. d.] . . . 4 . 1175
MISS Moore. G. M. Craik. 16°. New York, 1874 . . . . 4 . 874
MISSION (A) to Gelele, King of Dahome. R. F. Burton. 2 v. Sm. 8°. London, 1864 . . . . 13 . 141–42
MISTRESS of the Manse. J. G. Holland. 16°. New York, 1874. . . . 21 . 224
MODERN Christianity a civilized heathenism. By the author of "The fight at Dame Europa's school." 12°. Boston, 1875 . . . . . . 13 . 926
MODERN doubt and Christian belief. T. Christlieb. 8°. New York, 1874. 13 . 1317
MODERN saints and servants of God. 5 v. 8°. London, 1850–54 . . 13 . 915–19

Vol. I. Life of the venerable mother Margaret Mary Alacoque, Religieuse of the Order of the Visitation.
II. Lives of Margaret Mary Alacoque, and of St. Catherine of Bologna.
III. Life of St. Jane Frances de Chantal, foundress of the Order of the Visitation. Trans. from the French of Rev. Mother De Chaugy.
IV. Lives of St. Jane Frances de Chantal, St. Rose of Viterbo, and Blessed Mary of Oignies.
V. Life of St. Francis de Sales, Bishop and Prince of Geneva. Trans. from the Italian of Peter Hyacinth Gallitia.

MOFFAT, James C. A comparative history of religions. Part 2. Later scriptures; progress and revolutions of faith. 16°. New York, 1873 . . . . 13 . 173
MOLESWORTH, William Nassau. History of England from the year 1830–1874. 3 v. Sm. 8°. London, 1874 . . . . 13 . 164–66

Vol. I. Introductory; First introduction of the Reform bill; second introduction of the Reform bill; Reform bill carried; The first reformed parliament; Corporation reform.
II. Victoria regina; The income and property tax; The sliding scale; The anti-corn law league; The people's charter; The great exhibition.
III. Sebastopol; The Indian mutiny; The French treaty; The Palmerston ministry; The reform bill of 1867; The Gladstone ministry.

MONASTERY (The). *Sir* W. Scott. 2 v. in 1. 12°. Boston, 1873 . . . 4 . 225
MONEY-MAKER. W. T. Adams. 16°. Boston, 1874. . . . . 4 . 340
MONIKINS (The). J. F. Cooper. 12°. New York, 1873 . . . . 4 . 1055

MONROE, Lewis B., *editor*. Public and parlor readings: prose and poetry for the use of reading clubs and for public and social entertainment. Miscellaneous. 12°. Boston, 1872 . . . . 13 . 944
MONSIEUR Violet. F. Marryat. 12°. London, 1874 . . . . 4 . 251
MONSTERS (The) of the deep. W. H. D. Adams. 16°. London, 1875 . 13 . 960
MONTGOMERY, Florence. Thrown together. 16°. New York, 1872 . . 4 . 472
MOONFOLK. J. G. Austin. 8°. New York, 1874 . . . . 4 . 563
*MORAL essays. *Messieurs* du Port Royal. 4 v. in 2. London, 1724 . 13 . 879–80
MORAL (The) system. E. H. Gillett. Sm. 8°. New York, 1874 . . . 13 . 1140
MORE bedtime stories. L. C. Moulton. 16°. Boston, 1875 . . . . . . 4 . 371
MORFIT, Campbell. Chemical and pharmaceutic manipulations; a manual of the mechanical and chemico-mechanical operations of the laboratory, with 423 illustrations. 8°. Philadelphia, 1849 . . . . 13 . 1209
MORGAN, *Rev.* Henry. Ned Nevins, the newsboy; or, street-life in Boston. Illustrated. 16°. Boston, 1875 . . . . 4 . 839
MORLEY, Henry. A first sketch of English literature. Sm. 8°. London. [n. d.] . . . . 13 . 924
Memoirs of Bartholomew fair. With facsimile drawings, engraved upon wood. Sm. 8°. London [n. d.] . . . . 13 . 1171
MOROCCO, Adventures in, and journeys through the oases of Draa and Tafilet. *Dr.* Gerhard Rohlfs. 8°. London, 1874 . . . . 13 . 1351
MORRIS, William O'Connor. The French revolution and first empire; an historical sketch. Sm. 8°. London, 1874 . . . . 13 . 131
MOSAIC (The) worker's daughter. J. M. Capes. 3 v. Sm. 8°. London, 1868 . . . . 4 . 801–3
MOSCHELES, Charlotte, *editor*. Recent music and musicians as described in the diaries and correspondence of Ignatz Moscheles; and adapted from the original German by A. D. Coleridge. 16°. New York, 1874 . . . . 13 . 930
MOSE Evans. W. M. Baker. 12°. New York, 1874 . . . . 4 . 565
MOSS-SIDE. M. V. Terhune. 12°. New York, 1874 . . . . 4 . 1112
MOTHER-IN-LAW (The). E. D. E. N. Southworth. 12°. Philadelphia, 1860 . . . . 4 . 1031
MOTHERS (The) of great men. S. S. Ellis. Sm. 8°. London [n. d.] . . 13 . 111
MOTLEY, John Lothrop. The life and death of John of Barneveld, advocate of Holland; with a view of the primary causes and movements of the thirty years' war. With illustrations. 2 v. 8°. New York, 1874 . . . . 13 . 1412–13
MOUHOT, Henri. Travels in the central parts of Indo-China (Siam), Cambodia, and Laos, during the years 1858, 1859, and 1860. With illustrations. 2 v. 8°. London, 1864 . . . . 13 . 1348–49
MOULTON, Louise Chandler. More bedtime stories. Illustrated. 16°. Boston, 1875 . . . . 4 . 371
Some women's hearts. 16°. Boston, 1874 . . . . 4 . 372
MOUNTFORD, William. Euthanasy; or, happy talk towards the end of life. 12°. Boston, 1874 . . . . 13 . 922
MR. MIDSHIPMAN EASY. F. Marryat. 12°. London, 1873 . . . . . . 4 . 242
MRS. ARMINGTON'S ward; or, the inferior sex. Daniel Thew Wright. 16°. Boston, 1874 . . . . 4 . 837
MRS. SKAGGS's husbands. Bret Harte. 16°. Boston, 1874 . . . . . . 4 . 473

MUIRHEAD, James Patrick. The origin and progress of the mechanical inventions of James Watt, illustrated by his correspondence with his friends, and the specifications of his patents. 3 v. 8°. London, 1854 . . . . 13 . 1227–29

Contents. — Vol. I. Introductory memoir, and extracts from correspondence. Vol. II. Extracts from correspondence. Vol. III. Letters patent, specifications of patents, and appendix.

MULOCK, D. M. *See* CRAIK, Dinah Maria.
MUMMY (The). Jane W. London. 16°. London [n. d.] . . . . 4 . 846
MURRAY, Alexander S. Manual of mythology, for the use of schools, art-students, and general readers; founded on the works of Petiscus, Preller, and Welcker. With 35 plates on toned paper, representing 76 mythological subjects. Sm. 8°. London, 1873 . . . . 13 . 1169
MURRAY, John, *publisher.* A hand-book of Rome and its environs. 11th edition, carefully revised on the spot to the latest period. With a large plan of Rome, a map of the environs, &c. Sm. 8°. London, 1873 . . . . 13 . 1176
MURRAY, William Henry Harrison. Deacons. Illustrated. Sq. 16°. Boston, 1875 . . . . 4 . 555
MUSIC. Moscheles, Ignatz. Recent music and musicians. 16°. New York, 1874 . . . . 13 . 930
MY comrade's adventures in the highlands. H. Hinton. Sm. 8°. New York, 1874. 2 copies . . . . 4 . 915–16
MY life on the plains. *Gen.* G. A. Custer, U. S. A. 8°. New York, 1874. 13 . 1069
MY miscellanies. W. Collins. 12°. New York, 1874 . . . . 4 . 362
MY mother and I. D. M. Craik. Sm. 8°. New York, 1874 . . . . . 4 . 455
MY opinions and Betsey Bobbet's. M. Holley. 12°. Hartford, 1874. 2 copies . . . . 4 . 901–2
MY sister Jeannie. A. L. A. D. Dudevant. 16°. Boston, 1874 . . . . 4 . 835
*MYSTERIES of the court of London. G. W. M. Reynolds. 8°. Philadelphia [n. d.] . . . . 4 . 539
MYSTERIOUS (The) island. Part first. J. Verne. 12°. Boston, 1875. 2 copies . . . . 4 . 1232–33
MYSTERY (The) of Edwin Drood, and other stories. C. Dickens. 12°. Boston, 1871 . . . . 4 . 1319

N.

NAAKÉ, John T., *editor.* Slavonic fairy tales. Collected and translated from the Russian, Polish, Servian, and Bohemian. With illustrations. Sm. 8°. London, 1874 . . . . 4 . 1303
NAPOLEON III. Court and social life in France. Felix M. Whitehurst. 2 v. 8°. London, 1873 . . . . 13 . 1223–24
NARRATIVE of a journey through Central and Eastern Arabia. W. G. Palgrave. 2 v. 8°. London and Cambridge, 1865 . . . . . . 13 . 1220–21
NARRATIVE of travels and discoveries in Africa. D. Denham and H. Clapperton. 2 v. 8°. London, 1824 . . . . 13 . 1232–33

NASSAU, Mary Cloyd (Latta). Crowned in palm-land. A story of African mission life. Portrait. Illustrations. 12°. Philadelphia, 1874 . . 13 . 1157
NATURALIST (The) on the river Amazons. H. W. Bates. Sm. 8°. London, 1875 . . . . 13 . 934
NECROMANCER (The). G. W. M. Reynolds. 8°. Philadelphia [n. d.] . 4 . 543
NED Nevins; or, street-life in Boston. *Rev.* Henry Morgan. 16°. Boston, 1875 . . . . 4 . 839
NEMESIS. M. V. Terhune. 16°. New York, 1874 . . . . 4 . 1113
NEW, Charles. Life, wanderings, and labours in Eastern Africa: with an account of the first successful ascent of the equatorial snow mountain, Kilima Njaro; and remarks upon East African slavery. Portrait. Map and illustrations. Sm. 8°. London, 1874 . . . . 13 . 132
NEW (The) Hyperion. E. Shinn. 8°. Philadelphia, 1875 . . . . 4 . 522
NEWMAN, John Henry. Loss and gain: the story of a convert. Sm. 8°. London, 1874 . . . . 13 . 923
NEWTON Foster. F. Marryat. 12°. London, 1873 . . . . 4 . 243
NICHOLAS Nickleby. C. Dickens. 2 v. 12°. Boston, 1871 . . . . . 4 . 1320–21
NICHOLAS, Thomas. British ethnology. The pedigree of the English people: an argument, historical and scientific, on the formation and growth of the nation; tracing race-admixture in Britain from the earliest times, with especial reference to the incorporation of the Celtic aborigines. Maps and diagrams. Fourth edition. 8°. London, 1874. 13 . 1338

Note. — This edition is a reprint, without much alteration, of the Third Edition, for which the work had been carefully revised throughout. — *Preface.*

NICHOLSON, John. The operative mechanic and British machinist; being a practical display of the manufactories and mechanical arts of the United Kingdom. With a supplement relating to British public works, by Baron Dupin and Charles Taylor; and a further supplement by G. Finden Warr. Illustrated by above 150 engravings. Roy. 8°. London, 1853 . . . . 13 . 1402
NIMROD of the sea. W. M. Davis. 12°. New York, 1874 . . . . . . 4 . 363
NINA Gordon. H. B. Stowe. 2 v. in 1. 12°. Boston, 1874 . . . . . 4 . 355
NINETY-THREE. Victor Hugo. 8°. New York, 1874 . . . . 4 . 449
No alternative. A. Cudlip. Sm. 8°. Philadelphia [n. d.] 2 copies . 4 . 917–18
No moss. C. A. Fosdick. 16°. Cincinnati, 1870 . . . . 4 . 961
NOAD, Henry M. Chemical analysis, qualitative and quantitative, with numerous additions by Campbell Morfit. Illustrations. 8°. Philadelphia, 1849 . . . . 13 . 1208
NOBLE (A) lord. E. D. E. N. Southworth. 12°. Philadelphia [n. d.] . 4 . 1027
NORDHOFF, Charles. Northern California, Oregon, and the Sandwich Islands. Illustrated. 4°. New York, 1874 . . . . 13 . 1339
Politics for young Americans. Sm. 8°. N. Y., 1875. . . . . 13 . 939
NORMANDY, A. The commercial hand-book of chemical analysis. 12°. London, 1850 . . . . 13 . 849
NORSEMEN (The) in the west. R. M. Ballantyne. Sm. 8°. London, 1872. 4 . 1206
NORTH American review. 55 volumes with index. 8°. Boston, 1815–42. 16 . 401–56
Same. Vols. 118 and 119. 8°. Boston, 1874 . . . . 16 . 604–5

Note. — Volumes 56 to 117 of the North American review will be found in vol. 1 of the Catalogue (No. 16.501–59, 601–3).

NORTH and the south. H. Chase and C. W. Sanborn. 12°. Boston, 1856. 13 . 855
NORTHERN California, Oregon, and the Sandwich Islands. C. Nordhoff. 4°. New York, 1874 . . . . 13 . 1339
NORTHERN lands. W. T. Adams. 16°. Boston, 1873 . . . . 4 . 350
NORWOOD. H. W. Beecher. 12°. New York, 1874. 2 copies . . . . 4 . 905–6
NOT in their set. Marie Lenzen. 12°. Boston, 1874 . . . . 4 . 1140
NOW or never. W. T. Adams. 16°. Boston, 1875 . . . . 4 . 310
NURSERY noonings. M. A. Dodge. 16°. New York, 1875 . . . . . . 4 . 582

O.

OAK-OPENINGS. J. F. Cooper. 12°. New York, 1873 . . . . 4 . 1056
OCEAN (The) waifs. M. Reid. 16°. Boston, 1873 . . . . 4 . 1250
ODD people. M. Reid. 16°. Boston, 1874 . . . . 4 . 1251
O'DONOGHUE (The). C. Lever. Sm. 8°. London, 1872 . . . . 4 . 418
OFFICE (The) and duty of a Christian pastor. S. H. Tyng. 16°. New York, 1874 . . . . 13 . 138
OLD (The) curiosity shop. C. Dickens. 2 v. 12°. Boston, 1874 . . 4 . 1322–23
OLD-FASHIONED stories. T. Cooper. Sm. 8°. London, 1874 . . . . . . 4 . 463
OLD Mortality. *Sir* W. Scott. 2 v. in 1. 12°. Boston, 1873 . . . . 4 . 226
OLD-TIME pictures. B. F. Taylor. Sq. 16°. Boston, 1875 . . . . 21 . 232
OLD Rome and new Italy. E. Castelar. Sm. 8°. New York, 1874 . . 13 . 1270
OLD Saint Paul's. W. H. Ainsworth. 16°. London [n. d.] . . . . . . 4 . 1176
"OLD Shekarry" [*Pseud.*]. *See* LLOYD, H. A.
OLD (The) woman who lived in a shoe. A. M. Douglas. 16°. Boston, 1875. 4 . 572
OLIPHANT, Margaret (O. Wilson). A rose in June. [Fiction.] 8°. Boston, 1874 . . . . 4 . 525
OLIVER OPTIC [*Pseud.*]. *See* ADAMS, William T.
OLIVER Twist. C. Dickens. 12°. Boston, 1871 . . . . 4 . 1324
OLIVER Wyndham. Mrs. J. B. Webb. 16°. New York [n. d.] . . . . 4 . 878
OLLA podrida. F. Marryat. 12°. London, 1874 . . . . 4 . 249
ON a coral reef. J. A. Forbes. Sm. 8°. London [n. d.] . . . . 4 . 838
ON the eve. I. S. Turgénieff. 16°. New York, 1873. . . . . 4 . 872
ON time. W. T. Adams. 16°. Boston, 1875 . . . . 4 . 316
ONE of them. C. Lever. Sm. 8°. London, 1873 . . . . 4 . 419
ONWARD. J. A. Winscom. 16°. New York [n. d.] . . . . 4 . 439
OPENING of a chestnut burr. E. P. Roe. Sm. 8°. New York, 1874 . . 4 . 556
OPERATIVE mechanic, and British machinist. John Nicholson. Roy. 8°. London, 1853 . . . . 13 . 1402
O'REILLY, Eleanor Grace. The stories they tell me; or, Sue and I. Illustrated. 16°. New York, 1874 . . . . 4 . 480
ORIENTAL and linguistic studies. W. D. Whitney. 12°. New York, 1874. 13 . 1145
*ORIGINAL (The) lists of persons of quality, and emigrants who went from Great Britain to the American plantations, 1600–1700. Ed. by John Camden Hotten. 4°. London, 1874 . . . . 13 . 1546
OSCEOLA. M. Reid. 12°. New York, 1874. . . . . 4 . 1252

*OSGOOD'S middle states. A hand-book for travellers. A guide to the chief cities and popular resorts of the middle states, and to their scenery and historic attractions; with the northern frontier from Niagara Falls to Montreal; also, Baltimore, Washington, and Northern Virginia. With seven maps and fifteen plans. 12°. Boston, 1874. . 13 . 883

OSSOLI. Sarah Margaret Fuller, *marchesa d'*. At home and abroad; or, things and thoughts in America and Europe. Edited by her brother, Arthur B. Fuller. 12°. Boston, 1874. . . . . 13 . 127

Life without and life within; or, reviews, narratives, essays, and poems. Edited by A. B. Fuller. 12°. Boston, 1874 . . . . . . 13 . 128

Woman in the nineteenth century, and kindred papers relating to the sphere, condition, and duties of woman. Edited by A. B. Fuller. New and complete edition, with an introduction by Horace Greeley. 12°. Boston, 1874 . . . . 13 . 129

OTTLEY, W. Y. *See* ENGRAVINGS of the Marquis of Stafford.

"OUIDA" [*Pseud.*]. *See* RAME, Louisa de la.

OUR Fred. M. Finley. 16°. New York, 1874 . . . . 4 . 828

OUR Helen. R. S. Clarke. 16°. Boston, 1875. . . . . 4 . 840

OUR mutual friend. C. Dickens. 2 v. 12°. Boston, 1874 . . . . . 4 . 1325–26

OUR new crusade. E. E. Hale. Sq. 16°. Boston, 1875 . . . . 4 . 882

OUR pets; sketches of the furred and feathered favorites of the young. With numerous anecdotes illustrating their sagacity and affection. Illustrated with colored plates by A. F. Lydon. Sm. 8°. London [n. d.] 13 . 174

OUR Sunday school. Waldo Abbot. 12°. Boston, 1863 . . . . 13 . 877

OUTLAW'S (The) daughter. E. Bennett. 12°. Philadelphia, 1874 . . . 4 . 907

OUTLINES of cosmic philosophy. J. Fiske. 2 v. 8°. Boston, 1875 . 13 . 1258–59

OUTLINES of the world's history. W. Swinton. 8°. Boston, 1874 . . . 13 . 1177

OUTWARD bound. W. T. Adams. 16°. Boston, 1875 . . . . 4 . 343

OVER the ocean. Curtis Guild. 8°. Boston, 1875 . . . . 13 . 1250

OVINGDEAN grange. W. H. Ainsworth. 16°. London [n. d.] . . . . . 4 . 1177

OWEN, George W. The Leech club; or, the mysteries of the Catskills. 12°. Boston, 1874 . . . . 4 . 260

OWEN, Robert Dale. Footfalls on the boundary of another world. With narrative illustrations. 12°. Philadelphia, 1874 . . . . 13 . 1269

OXENFORD, John, *translator*. Conversations of Goethe with Eckermann and Soret. Sm. 8°. London, 1874 . . . . 13 . 112

OXFORD and Cambridge boat races. W. F. Macmichael. Sm. 8°. Cambridge, 1870 . . . . 13 . 876

P.

PACHA (The) of many tales. F. Marryat. 12°. London, 1873 . . . . 4 . 244

PAINTERS, sculptors, architects, engravers, and their works. C. E. Clement. Sm. 8°. New York, 1874 . . . . 13 . 146

PAINTING, A concise history of. *Mrs.* C. Heaton. Sm. 8°. Lond., 1874. 13 . 925

PALACE and cottage. W. T. Adams. 16°. Boston, 1875 . . . . 4 . 347

PALGRAVE, William Gifford. Personal narrative of a year's journey through Central and Eastern Arabia (1862–63). Portrait. Folded map and plans. 2 v. 8°. London, 1865 . . . . 13 . 1220–21

PALMER, Ray. Earnest words on true success in life, addressed to young men and women. 16°. New York and Chicago, 1873 . . . . . . 13 . 169

PARACLETE (The). An essay on the personality and ministry of the Holy Ghost, with some reference to current discussions. 8°. New York, 1875 . . . . 13 . 1134

PARDEE, Richard Gay. The sabbath school index. 16°. Philadelphia, 1868 . . . . 13 . 875

PARISIANS (The). E. G. E. L. Bulwer. 2 v. in 1. 12°. New York, 1874. 4 . 481

Another edition. 3 v. in 1. 16°. Philadelphia, 1874 . . . . 4 . 482

PARKMAN, Francis. The old régime in Canada, 1653 to 1763. 8°. Boston, 1874 . . . . 13 . 1138

PARR, Harriet. [*Holme Lee.*] The vicissitudes of Bessie Fairfax. A novel. 16°. Philadelphia [n. d.] . . . . 4 . 356

PARR, Louisa. Hero Carthew. 16°. New York, 1873 . . . . 4 . 870

PARSON'S (The) daughter. T. Hook. 16°. London [n. d.] . . . . . . 4 . 818

PARTERRE (The) of fiction, poetry, history, literature, and the fine arts. With illustrations. 5 v. 8°. London, 1834–36 . . . . 4 . 549–53

Note.—"The Parterre" is a collection of short sketches and stories by many different writers.

PARTON, James. Life of Thomas Jefferson. Portrait. 8°. Boston, 1874. 13 . 1249

PASSION and principle. T. Hook. 16°. London [n. d.] . . . . 4 . 819

PASSIONS. A book of the passions. Illustrated. G. P. R. James. 8°. London, 1839 . . . . 13 . 1231

PATHFINDER (The). J. F. Cooper. 12°. New York, 1874 . . . . . . 4 . 1057

PATRICIA Kemball. E. L. Linton. 12°. Philadelphia, 1875. 2 copies. 4 . 923–24

PAUL Prescott's charge. H. Alger, jun. 16°. Boston, 1865 . . . . . 4 . 1145

PAUL the peddler. H. Alger, jun. 16°. Boston, 1871 . . . . 4 . 1162

PAYN, James. The family scapegrace; or, Richard Arbour. Sm. 8°. London [n. d.] . . . . 4 . 569

PEABODY, Andrew P. Christianity and science. A series of lectures delivered in New York, in 1874, on the Ely foundation of the Union Theological Seminary. Sm. 8°. New York, 1874 . . . . 13 . 937

PEABODY, E. P. Record of Mr. Alcott's school, exemplifying the principles and methods of moral culture. 16°. Boston, 1874 . . . . 13 . 179

PEAKE, Elizabeth. Pen pictures of Europe. Illustrations. 8°. Philadelphia, 1874 . . . . 13 . 1137

PEDIGREE (The), of the English people. Thomas Nicholas. 8°. London, 1874 . . . . 13 . 1338

PEG Woffington, Christie Johnstone, and other stories. C. Reade. Sm. 8°. Boston, 1873 . . . . 4 . 1125

The same. Sm. 8°. Boston, 1875 . . . . 4 . 1126

PEIRCE, C. H. Examinations of drugs, medicines, chemicals, &c., as to their purity and adulterations. 12°. Philadelphia, 1853 . . . . 13 . 848

PEN pictures of Europe. E. Peake. 8°. Philadelphia, 1874 . . . . . 13 . 1137

PERCIVAL Keene. F. Marryat. 12°. London [n. d.] . . . . 4 . 245

PEREGRINE Bunce. T. Hook. 16°. London [n. d.] . . . . 4 . 820

PERIODICALS. American journal of science and arts, 3d series. Vols. 7 and 8. 8°. New Haven, 1874 . . . . 18 . 1462–63
Atlantic monthly. Vols. 33 and 34. 8°. Boston, 1874 . . . . . 20 . 433–34
Blackwood's magazine. Vols. 115 and 116. 8°. New York, 1874. 18 . 1306–7
Eclectic magazine. Vols. 19 and 20. New series. 8°. New York, 1874 . . . . 19 . 630–31
Harper's monthly magazine. Vols. 48 and 49. 8°. New York, 1874 . . . . 12 . 101–2
International review. Vol. 1. 8°. New York, 1874 . . . . 12 . 201
Journal of the Franklin institute. Vols. 67 and 68. 8°. Philadelphia, 1874. . . . . 17 . 463–64
Littell's living age. Vols. 117 to 123, inclusive. 8°. Boston, 1873–74 . . . . 12 . 1–7
North American review. First 55 volumes with index. 8°. Boston, 1815–1842 . . . . 16 . 401–56
Same. Vols. 118 and 119. 8°. Boston, 1874 . . . . 16 . 604–5
*Scientific American. Vols. 12 to 31 inclusive. Folio. New York, 1865–74 . . . . 12 . 712–31
St. Nicholas magazine. Vol. 1. 8°. New York, 187 4 12–301

PERRY, Nora. After the ball, and other poems. 16°. Boston, 1875 . . 21 . 247

PERSONAL recollections of Mary Somerville. Martha Somerville. 8°. Boston, 1874 . . . . 13 . 1257

PERSONAL reminiscences, by Chorley, Planché, and Young. Ed. by R. S. Stoddard. 16°. New York, 1874 . . . . 13 . 971

PERU, Two years in. Thomas J. Hutchinson. Map and illustrations. 2 v. 8°. London, 1873. . . . . 13 . 1225–26

PET; or, pastimes and penalties. H. R. Haweis. 12°. New York, 1874 . 4 . 566

PETER the Great, emperor of Russia. J. Abbott. 16°. New York, 1874 . 13 . 878

PETER Simple. F. Marryat. 12°. London, 1873 . . . . 4 . 246

PETTIGREW, Thomas Joseph. On superstitions connected with the history and practice of medicine and surgery. 8°. London, 1844 . . . . 13 . 1234

PEVERIL of the peak. *Sir* W. Scott. 2 v. in 1. 12°. Boston, 1874 . . 4 . 227

PHANTASMION. Sara Coleridge. 12°. Boston, 1874. . . . . 4 . 1073

PHANTOM (The) of the forest. E. Bennett. 12°. Philadelphia, 1867 . . 4 . 908

PHANTOM (The) ship. F. Marryat. 12°. London, 1874 . . . . 4 . 247

*PHARMACOGRAPHIA. A history of drugs. F. A. Flückiger, and Daniel Hanbury. 8°. London, 1874 . . . . 13 . 1550

PHELPS, Lavinia Howe. Dramatic stories for home and school entertainment. 12°. Chicago, 1874 . . . . 21 . 223

PHEMIE Frost's experiences. A. S. Stephens. 12°. New York, 1874 . . 4 . 357

PHEMIE's temptation. M. V. Terhune. 12°. New York, 1874 . . . . 4 . 1114

PHENIX (The). A collection of choice, scarce, and valuable tracts, being taken from MSS. and printed books, very uncommon, and not to be found but in the libraries of the curious. By a gentleman who has searched after them for above twenty years. 2 v. 8°. London, 1708–21 . . . . 13 . 852–53

PHIL the fiddler. H. Alger, jun. 16°. Boston, 1872 . . . . 4 . 1163

*PHILLIPS, J. Arthur. Elements of metallurgy. A practical treatise on the art of extracting metals from their ores. Illustrations. Roy. 8°. London, 1874 . . . . 13 . 1549

PHILOLOGY of the English tongue. J. Earle. Sm. 8°. London, 1873. . 13 . 868
PHINEAS Redux. Anthony Trollope. 8°. New York, 1874 . . . . . 4 . 528
PHYSICIAN'S (The) daughters; or, the spring-time of woman. A tale. 16°. New York [n. d.] . . . . 4 . 938
PHYSIOLOGY for practical use. J. Hinton. Sm. 8°. New York, 1874 . . 13 . 1266
PICKWICK papers. C. Dickens. 2 v. 12°. Boston, 1875 . . . . . 4 . 1327–28
PICTURES from Italy, and American notes. C. Dickens. 12°. Boston, 1871 . . . . 4 . 1329
PIERCE, Edward L. Index of the special railroad laws of Massachusetts. 1826–73. 8°. Boston, 1874 . . . . 11 . 1250
PILGRIM (The) fathers of New England. W. Carlos Martyn. 12°. New York, 1867 . . . . 13 . 171
PILOT (The). J. F. Cooper. 12°. New York, 1872 . . . . 4 . 1058
*PINDAR, Peter, The works of, with a copious index. To which is prefixed some account of his life. 4 v. 24°. London, 1816 . . . 21 . 256–59
PINKERTON, Allan. The expressman and the detective. 16°. Chicago, 1874 . . . . 4 . 975
PIONEERS (The). J. F. Cooper. 12°. New York, 1875 . . . . . . 4 . 1059
PIRATE (The). *Sir* W. Scott. 2 v. in 1. 12°. Boston, 1873 . . . . 4 . 228
PIRATE (The) city. R. M. Ballantyne. 16°. New York, 1874. 2 copies. 4 . 1207–8
PIRATE'S (The) treasure, and other tales. W. H. G. Kingston. 16°. New York, 1869 . . . . 4 . 932
PLANE and plank. W. T. Adams. 16°. Boston, 1875 . . . . 4 . 327
PLANT-HUNTERS (The). M. Reid. 16°. Boston, 1874 . . . . 4 . 1253
PLAYS and puritans. C. Kingsley. Sm. 8°. London, 1873 . . . . . 13 . 102
PLEASANT talk about fruits, flowers, and farming. H. W. Beecher. 12°. New York, 1874 . . . . 13 . 156
POACHER (The). F. Marryat. 12°. London [n. d.] . . . . 4 . 248
POEMS. Aikin, Lucy. Epistles on woman, with miscellaneous poems. 12°. Boston, 1810 . . . . 21 . 251
Austin, Mrs. G. L., *editor*. Little people of God. 16°. Boston, 1874. 21 . 229
Baker, George M., *editor*. Ballads of beauty. Sm. 4°. Boston, 1875. 21 . 209
Blake, William. Poetical works, lyrical and miscellaneous. Edited, with a prefatory memoir, by William Michael Rossetti. Portrait. 16°. Boston, 1875 . . . . 21 . 248
Browning, Robert. Sordello. 16°. London, 1840 . . . . 21 . 236
Bulwer-Lytton, (Edward) Robert. Fables in song. 16°. Boston, 1874. 21 . 250
Calverley, C. S. Fly leaves. 16°. New York, 1872 . . . . 21 . 249
Chapman, George. Works. Sm. 8°. London, 1874 . . . . 21 . 227
Child, Francis James, *editor*. English and Scottish ballads. 8 v. Sm. 8°. Boston, 1860 . . . . 21 . 214–21
Clarke, Mary C. The trust and the remittance. 16°. Boston, 1874 . 21 . 238
Colman, James F. The knightly heart, and other poems. 16°. Boston, 1873 . . . . 21 . 230
De Vere, Aubrey. Legends of Saint Patrick. Sm. 8°. London, 1872. 21 . 237
Dodge, Mary M. Rhymes and jingles. 16°. New York, 1875 . . 21 . 228
Furness, Helen K. A concordance to Shakspeare's poems. Roy. 8°. Philadelphia, 1874 . . . . 21 . 204
Harte, (Francis) Bret. Echoes of the foot-hills. 16°. Boston, 1875 . 21 . 244
Hillhouse, James A. Dramas. 2 v. 16°. Boston, 1839 . . . . 21 . 233–34

POEMS (*continued*).
Holland, J. G. Mistress of the manse. 16°. New York, 1874 . . 21 . 224
Holmes, O. W. Songs of many seasons. 1862–1874. 16°. Boston, 1875. 21 . 245
Jamieson, Robert, *editor*. Popular ballads and songs from ancient MSS. 2 v. 8°. Edinburgh, 1806 . . . . 21 . 211–12
Larcom, L. Childhood songs. Sq. 8°. Boston, 1875 . . . . 21 . 226
Leyden, John. Poetical remains. 8°. London, 1819 . . . . 21 . 210
Milton, John. Poetical work. Edited with introductions, notes, and an essay on Milton's English, by David Masson. Portrait. 3 v. 8°. London, 1874 . . . . 21 . 206–8
Perry, Nora. After the ball, and other poems. 16°. Boston, 1875. 21 . 247
Phelps, L. H. Dramatic stories. 12°. Chicago, 1874 . . . . . . 21 . 223
*Pindar, Peter. Works. 4 v. 24°. London, 1816 . . . . . . 21 . 256–59
Putnam, Alfred P. Singers and songs. 8°. Boston, 1875 . . . . 21 . 213
Quiet hours. 18°. Boston, 1874 . . . . 21 . 255
Sheridan, R. B. Works. Sm. 8°. London, 1874 . . . . 21 . 225
Stoddard, W. O. Verses for many days. 16°. New York, 1874 . . 21 . 231
Swinburne, A. C. Bothwell. Sm. 8°. London, 1874 . . . . 21 . 222
Tannahill, R., and Wilson, J. Poetical works. 2 v. in 1. 12°. London 1851. . . . . 21 . 253
Taylor, Benjamin F. Old-time pictures, and sheaves of rhyme. Illustrated. Sq. 16°. Chicago, 1875 . . . . 21 . 232
Trowbridge, John T. Emigrant's (The) story, and other poems. 16°. Boston, 1875 . . . . 21 . 246
Whittier, J. G. Hazel-blossoms. 16°. Boston, 1875 . . . . 21 . 243
POLITICAL economy. J. E. Cairns. 8°. New York, 1874 . . . . 13 . 1341
POLITICAL economy, Principles of. John Stuart Mill. 2 v. 8°. Boston, 1848 . . . . 13 . 1423–24
POLITICS for young Americans. C. Nordhoff. Sm. 8°. New York, 1875. 13 . 939
POOR and proud. W. T. Adams. 16°. Boston, 1875 . . . . 4 . 312
POPULAR ballads and songs, from ancient MSS. Ed. by Robert Jamieson. 2 v. 8°. Edinburgh, 1806 . . . . 21 . 211–12
*PORT Royal, *Messieurs* du. Moral essays contain'd in several treatises, on many important duties. 4 v. in 2. 12°. London, 1724 . . . 13 . 879–80
PORTER, Rose. The Winter fire. *A sequel* to "Summer drift-wood." 16°. New York, 1874 . . . . 4 . 829
PORTRAIT. (The) A. G. Riddle. 12°. Boston, 1874 . . . . 4 . 471
POSTHUMOUS papers of L. Nathaniel Rossel. 8°. London, 1872 . . . 13 . 119
POWER, *Mrs.* S. D. The ugly-girl papers; or, hints for the toilet. Sq. 16°. New York, 1875 . . . . 4 . 877
PRAIRIE (The). J. F. Cooper. 12°. New York, 1873 . . . . 4 . 1060
PRAIRIE and forest. P. Gillmore. 12°. New York, 1874 . . . . . . 13 . 1152
PRAYER and the prayer gauge. M. Hopkins. 16°. New York [n. d.] . . 13 . 175
PRE-ADAMITE (The). A. Hoyle Lester. 16°. Philadelphia, 1875 . . . 13 . 1159
PRECAUTION. J. F. Cooper. 12°. New York, 1873 . . . . 4 . 1061
PRENTISS, Elizabeth. Urbané and his friends. 12°. New York, 1874 . . 4 . 557
*PRESENT (The) state of the Cape of Good Hope. Peter Kolben. 8°. London, 1731 . . . . 13 . 913
PRETTY Mrs. Gaston, and other stories. John E. Cooke. 16°. New York, 1874. . . . . 4 . 457

PRIME, Samuel Irenæus. Under the trees. Sm. 8°. New York, 1874 . . 13 . 1243
PRIMITIVE culture. E. B. Tylor. 2 v. 8°. Boston, 1874 . . . 13 . 1065–66
PRINCE (The) of darkness. E. D. E. N. Southworth. 12°. Philadelphia, 1869. 4 . 1032
PRINCESS (The) of Silverland, by Elsie Strivelyne [*Pseud.*]. Sm. 8°. London, 1874 . . . . 4 . 832
PRINCESS (A) of Thule. W. Black. Sm. 8°. London, 1874 . . . . 4 . 264
PRINCIPLES of geology. *See* LYELL, Sir Charles.
*PRINTS. King Charles I., and the heads of the noble earls, lords, and others who suffered for their loyalty in the rebellion and civil-wars of England (1649). With their characters engraved under each print, extracted from *Lord* Clarendon. Taken from original pictures, many of them *Sir* Anthony Vandyke's. Engraved by George Vertue. 11 plates. 4°. London, 1746 . . . . 13 . 1516
PROBLEMS of life and mind. G. H. Lewes. Vol. 1. 8°. Boston, 1874 . 13 . 1256
PROCTOR, Richard Anthony. The expanse of heaven: a series of essays on the wonders of the firmament. 12°. New York, 1874 . . . . . 13 . 929
PROFFATT, John. Woman before the law. 16°. New York, 1874 . . . 13 . 1160
PROGRESSIVE petticoats. R. B. Roosevelt. 12°. New York, 1874 . . . 4 . 470
PROPHETIC voices concerning America. Charles Sumner. 8°. Boston, 1874 13 . 1251
PROSE idyls, new and old. Charles Kingsley. Sm. 8°. London, 1873 . 13 . 103
PROSPER. V. Cherbuliez. 16°. New York, 1874 . . . . 4 . 859
PRUDENCE Palfrey. T. B. Aldrich. 16°. Boston, 1875 . . . . . . 4 . 573
PSALMS, A translation and commentary of the book of. Augustus Tholuck, D.D. 12°. Philadelphia, 1858 . . . . 13 . 1238
PUBLIC and parlor readings. Miscellaneous. Ed. by L. B. Monroe. 12°. Boston, 1872 . . . . 13 . 944
PUDDLEFORD (The) papers. H. H. Riley. Sm. 8°. Boston, 1875 . . . 4 . 584
PUT yourself in his place. C. Reade. Sm. 8°. Boston, 1874 . . . . 4 . 1127
PUTNAM, Alfred Porter, *editor*. Singers and songs of the liberal faith; being selections of hymns and other sacred poems of the liberal church in America, with biographical sketches of the writers, and with historical and illustrative notes. 8°. Boston, 1875 . . . . 21 . 213
PYRENEES, A tour through the. H. A. Taine. 12°. New York, 1874. . 13 . 1260

Q.

QUADROON (The). M. Reid. 12°. New York, 1874 . . . . 4 . 1255
*QUAIN, Jones, and WILSON, W. J. E. A series of anatomical plates, with references and physiological comments, illustrating the structure of the different parts of the human body. American edition revised, with additional notes by Joseph Pancoast, M. D. 4°. Philadelphia, 1852 13 . 1504
QUENTIN Durward. *Sir* W. Scott. 2 v. in 1. 12°. Boston, 1868 . . . 4 . 229
QUIET hours. A collection of poems by different authors. 18°. Boston, 1874. 21 . 235

R.

RAE, W. F. Wilkes, Sheridan, Fox. The opposition under George the third. 12°. New York, 1874 . . . . 13 . 935
RAGGED Dick. H. Alger, jun. 16°. Boston, 1868 . . . . 4 . 1154

RAMBLE (A) round the world, 1871. J. A. Von Hübner. 8°. New York, 1874 . . . . 13 . 932
RAME, Louise de la. [*Ouida.*] Bébée; or, two little wooden shoes. 12°. Philadelphia, 1874 . . . . 4 . 1141
RAN away to sea. M. Reid. 16°. Boston, 1872 . . . . 4 . 1256
The same. 16°. Boston, 1874 . . . . 4 . 1257
RANDOLPH, *Mrs.* ——. Gentianella. (A novel.) Sm. 8°. Philadelphia [n. d.] . . . . 4 . 1072
RANGERS (The) and regulators of the Tanaha. M. Reid. 12°. New York, 1874 . . . . 4 . 1258
RANKIN, Fannie Wolcott. True to him ever. A novel. Sm. 8°. New York, 1874 . . . . 4 . 980
RATTLIN the reefer. Ed. by F. Marryat. 12°. London, 1873 . . . . . 4 . 250
RAWLINSON, George. The five great monarchies of the ancient eastern world; or, the history, geography, and antiquities of Chaldæa, Assyria, Babylon, Media, and Persia, collected and illustrated from ancient and modern sources. Second edition. With maps and illustrations. 3 v. 8°. New York, 1871. . . . . 13 . 1326–28
Historical illustrations of the Old Testament. With additions by H. B. Hackett. 16°. Boston, 1873. . . . . 13 . 1173
REYNAL, F. E. Wrecked on a reef; or, twenty months among the Auckland isles. A true story. 40 illustrations. Sm. 8°. London, 1874 . . 4 . 263
READE, Charles. The cloister and the hearth; or, maid, wife, and widow. A matter-of-fact romance. Sm. 8°. Boston, 1872. . . . . 4 . 1118
Foul play. A novel, by Charles Reade and Dion Boucicault. Sm. 8°. Boston, 1874 . . . . 4 . 1119
Griffith Gaunt; or, jealousy. Sm. 8°. Boston, 1875. 2 copies . 4 . 1120–21
Hard cash. A matter-of-fact romance. Sm. 8°. Boston, 1874 . . . 4 . 1122
"Love me little, Love me long." Sm. 8°. Boston, 1875 . . . . . . 4 . 1123
It is never too late to mend. A matter-of-fact romance. Sm. 8°. Boston, 1874. . . . . 4 . 1124
Peg Woffington, Christie Johnstone, and other stories. Sm. 8°. Boston, 1873. . . . . 4 . 1125

Contents. — Peg Woffington; Christie Johnstone; Clouds and sunshine; Art, a dramatic tale; Propria quæ maribus; The box tunnel; Jack of all trades.

The Same. Sm. 8°. Boston, 1875 . . . . 4 . 1126
Put yourself in his place. Sm. 8°. Boston, 1874 . . . . 4 . 1127
A simpleton, and The wandering heir. Sm. 8°. Boston, 1873 . . . 4 . 1128
A terrible temptation. Sm. 8°. Boston, 1872 . . . . 4 . 1129
White lies. A novel. Sm. 8°. Boston, 1872. . . . . 4 . 1130
READING club (The) and handy speaker. Ed. by G. M. Baker. 16°. Boston, 1874. . . . . 21 . 242
REASONING, Easy lessons in. Richard Whately. 12°. Boston, 1852 . . 13 . 140
REBEL'S (A) recollections. G. C. Eggleston. 16°. New York, 1875 . . 4 . 578
RECENT art and society. H. F. Chorley. Sm. 8°. New York, 1874 . . 13 . 1267
RECOLLECTIONS of a tour made in Scotland A.D. 1803, by Dorothy Wordsworth. Ed. by J. C. Shairp. Sm. 8°. New York, 1874 . . . . 13 . 955
RECORD of Mr. Alcott's school. E. P. Peabody. 16°. Boston, 1874 . . 13 . 179

RED cross. W. T. Adams. 16°. Boston, 1875 . . . . 4 . 345
RED (The) rover. J. F. Cooper. 12°. New York, 1872 . . . . 4 . 1062
REDGAUNTLET. *Sir* W. Scott. 2 v. in 1. 12°. Boston, 1872 . . . . 4 . 230
REDSKINS (The). J. F. Cooper. 12°. New York, 1873 . . . . 4 . 1044
REES, James. Life of Edwin Forrest; with reminiscences and personal recollections. Portrait. 12°. Philadelphia, 1874 . . . . 13 . 133
*REFLECTOR (The): representing human affairs, as they are; and may be improved. 8°. London, 1750 . . . . 13 . 845
REID, *Captain* Mayne. Afloat in the forest; or, a voyage among the tree-tops. Illustrated. 16°. Boston, 1873 . . . . 4 . 1237
The boy hunters; or, adventures in search of a white buffalo. Illustrated. 16°. Boston, 1874 . . . . 4 . 1238
The boy slaves. Illustrated. 16°. Boston, 1874 . . . . 4 . 1239
The boy tar; or, a voyage in the dark. Illustrated. 16°. Boston, 1874 . . . . 4 . 1240
Bruin: the grand bear hunt. Illustrated. 16°. Boston, 1872 . . 4 . 1241
The bush-boys; or, the history and adventures of a Cape farmer and his family in the wild Karoos of Southern Afriça. Illustrated. 16°. Boston, 1874 . . . . 4 . 1242
The desert home; or, the adventures of a lost family in the wilderness. Illustrated. 16°. Boston, 1872 . . . . 4 . 1243
The forest exiles; or, the perils of a Peruvian family amid the wilds of the Amazon. Illustrated. 16°. Boston, 1874 . . . . . . 4 . 1244
The giraffe-hunters. Illustrated. 16°. Boston, 1873 . . . . 4 . 1245
The headless horseman. Illustrated. 12°. New York, 1874 . . . 4 . 1246
The hunter's feast; or, conversations around the camp fire. Illustrated. 12°. New York, 1874 . . . . 4 . 1247
Lost Lenore, Illustrated. 12°. New York, 1874 . . . . 4 . 1248
The maroon; or, planter life in Jamaica. Illustrated. 12°. New York, 1874 . . . . 4 . 1249
The ocean-waifs; a story of adventure on land and sea. Illustrated. 16°. Boston, 1873 . . . . 4 . 1250
Odd people; being a popular description of singular races of man. Illustrated. 16°. Boston, 1874 . . . . 4 . 1251
Osceola, the Seminole; or, the red fawn of the flower land. Illustrated. 12°. New York, 1874 . . . . 4 . 1252
The plant-hunters; or, adventures among the Himalaya mountains. Illustrated. 16°. Boston, 1874 . . . . 4 . 1253
The cliff-climbers; or, the lone home in the Himalayas. *A sequel* to "The plant-hunters." Illustrated. 16°. Boston, 1874 . . . . 4 . 1254
The quadroon; or, a lover's adventures in Louisiana. Illustrated. 12°. New York, 1874 . . . . 4 . 1255
Ran away to sea: an autobiography for boys. Illustrated. 16°. Boston, 1872 . . . . 4 . 1256
The same. 16°. Boston, 1874 . . . . 4 . 1257
The rangers and regulators of the Tanaha; or, life among the lawless. A tale of the republic of Texas. Illustrated. 12°. New York, 1874 . . . . 4 . 1258
The rifle-rangers; or, adventures in southern Mexico. Illustrated. 12°. New York, 1874 . . . . 4 . 1259

REID, M. (*continued*).

The scalp-hunters; or, adventures among the trappers. Illustrated. 12°. New York, 1874 . . . . 4 . 1260

The tiger-hunter; or, a hero in spite of himself. Illustrated. 12°. New York, 1874. . . . . 4 . 1261

The war-trail; or, the hunt of the wild horse. A romance of the prairie. Illustrated. 12°. New York, 1874 . . . . 4 . 1262

The white chief. A legend of North Mexico. Illustrated. 12°. New York, 1874 . . . . 4 . 1263

The white gauntlet. Illustrated. 12°. New York, 1874 . . . . . . 4 . 1264

The wild huntress; or, love in the wilderness. Illustrated. 12°. New York, 1874 . . . . 4 . 1265

Wild life; or, adventures on the frontier. A tale of the early days of the Texan republic. Illustrated. 12°. New York, 1874 . . . . . 4 . 1266

The wood-rangers; or, the trappers of Sonora. Illustrated. 12°. New York, 1874 . . . . 4 . 1267

The young voyageurs; or, the boy hunters in the north. Illustrated. 16°. Boston, 1874 . . . . 4 . 1268

The young yägers; or, a narrative of hunting adventures in Southern Africa. Illustrated. 16°. Boston, 1874. . . . . 4 . 1269

*REJECTION of the miracles by the heathens. W. Weston. 8°. Cambridge, 1746 . . . . 13 . 843

*RELIQUÆ Wottonianæ; or, a collection of lives, letters, poems; with characters of sundry personages; and other incomparable pieces of language and art. *Sir* Henry Wotton. Sm. 8°. London, 1651 . . . 13 . 891

REMARKABLE (The) adventures of celebrated persons, embracing adventures of persons eminent in the history of Europe and America. 12°. New York, 1855 . . . . 4 . 258

RENDU, Louis. Théorie des glaciers de la Savoie. 8°. Chambéry, 1840. 13 . 1330

Theory of the glaciers of Savoy. Trans. by A. Wills. To which are added the original memoir, and supplementary articles by P. G. Tait, and John Ruskin. Edited with introductory remarks by George Forbes. 1 plate. 8°. London, 1874 . . . . .13 . 1330

Note.—This book is published] in the interests of Principal Forbes claims to be considered as the originator of the viscous or plastic theory of glaciers. Prof. Tyndall, in his "Glaciers of the Alps" [19.1138], had assigned a prior claim to Bishop Rendu. See a popular statement of Forbes glacial theory in Littell's Living Age, vol. 120, p. 247 [12.4].

RENT (A) in a cloud, and St. Patrick's eve. C. Lever. Sm. 8°. London, [n. d.] . . . . 4 . 420

REPORT of the superintendent of the United States Coast Survey, showing the progress of the survey during the year 1870. 4°. Washington, 1873 . . . . 11 . 751

REPORT on observations of the total eclipse of the sun, Aug. 7, 1869. *Com.* B. F. Sands, U. S. N. 4°. Washington, 1870 . . . . 11 . 752

RETRIBUTION. E. D. E. N Southworth. 12°. Philadelphia, 1856 . . . 4 . 1033

REVERE, Joseph Warren. Keel and saddle: a retrospect of forty years of military and naval service. 12°. Boston, 1873. . . . . .13 . 1155

RÉVOIL, Benedict. The hunter and the trapper in North America; or, romantic adventures in field and forest. Trans. from the French by W. H. D. Adams. 16°. London, 1874. 2 copies . . . . . . 4 . 925-26
REYNOLDS, George W. M. Joseph Wilmot; or, the memoirs of a manservant. 8°. Philadelphia [n. d.] . . . . 4 . 532
The banker's daughter. *A sequel* to "Joseph Wilmot." 8°. Philadelphia [n. d.] . . . . 4 . 533
Kenneth, the earl of Glengyle. 8°. Philadelphia [n. d.] . . . . . . 4 . 534
Lord Saxondale; or, life among the London aristocracy. 8°. Philadelphia [n. d.] . . . . 4 . 535
Count Christoval. *A sequel* to "Lord Saxondale." 8°. Philadelphia [n. d.] . . . . 4 . 536
Mary Price; or, the adventures of a servant-maid. 8°. Philadelphia [n. d.] . . . . 4 . 537
Eustace Quentin. *A sequel* to "Mary Price." 8°. Philadelphia [n. d.] . . . . 4 . 538
*Mysteries of the court of London. 8°. Philadelphia [n. d.] . . . 4 . 539
*Rose Foster; or, the "second series" of the Mysteries of the court of London. 8°. Philadelphia [n. d.] . . . . 4 . 540
*Caroline of Brunswick; or, the "third series" of the Mysteries of the court of London. 8°. Philadelphia [n. d.] . . . . 4 . 541
*Venictia Trelawney; or, the "fourth series" "and final conclusion" of the Mysteries of the court of London. 8°. Philadelphia [n. d.]. 4 . 542
The necromancer; or, the mysteries of the court of Henry the Eighth. 8°. Philadelphia [n. d.] . . . . 4 . 543
Rosa Lambert; or, the memoirs of an unfortunate woman. 8°. Philadelphia [n. d.] . . . . 4 . 544
The Rye-house plot; or, Ruth, the conspirator's daughter. 8°. Philadelphia [n. d] . . . . 4 . 545
RHINE (The). Victor Hugo. 16°. Boston [n. d.] . . . . 13 . 161
*RHODE Island, Atlas of the State of, and Providence Plantations, from actual surveys and official records: compiled by D. G. Beers and Co. Roy. 4°. Philadelphia, 1870 . . . . 15 . 1420
RHYMES and jingles. Mary M. Dodge. 16°. New York, 1875 . . . . 21 . 4228
RICH and humble. W. T. Adams. 16°. Boston, 1875 . . . . 4 . 332
*RICHARDSON, Charles. A new dictionary of the English language, combining explanation with etymology, and illustrated by quotations from the best authorities. 2 v. 4°. London, 1867. Vol. 1, A-K; Vol. 2, L-Z.. . . . . 13 . 1511-12
RIDDLE, A. G. The portrait: a romance of the Cuyahoga valley. 12°. Boston, 1874 . . . . 4 . 471
RIFLE-RANGERS (The). M. Reid. 12°. New York, 1874 . . . . . 4 . 1259
RILEY, Henry Hopkins. The Puddleford papers; or, humors of the West. With illustrations. Sm. 8°. Boston, 1875 . . . . 4 . 584
RISEN from the ranks. H. Alger, jun. 16°. Boston, 1874 . . . . . . 4 . 1153
RISING (The) faith. C. A. Bartol. 16°. Boston, 1874 . . . . 13 . 964
ROB Roy. *Sir* W. Scott. 2 v. in 1. 12. Boston, 1874 . . . . 4 . 231
ROBBINS, Sarah C. Doors outward. A tale. (Juvenile.) 16°. New York, 1875. 4 . 850
ROBINSON, W. The subtropical garden; or, beauty of form in the flower garden. With illustrations. Sm. 8°. London, 1871. . . . . . . 13 . 113

ROCK, Daniel. The church of our fathers, as seen in St. Osmund's rite for the cathedral of Salisbury; with dissertations on the belief and ritual in England before and after the coming of the Normans. 4 v. 8°. London, 1849 . . . . 13 . 1056–59

ROE, Edward P. Opening of a chestnut burr. Sm. 8°. New York, 1874. 4 . 556

ROGERS, Henry. The superhuman origin of the Bible inferred from itself. Sm. 8°. New York, 1874 . . . . 13 . 1354

ROGERS, Nathaniel Peabody, Collections from the miscellaneous writings of. 12°. Boston, 1849 . . . . 13 . 851

ROHLFS, *Dr.* Gerhard. Adventures in Morocco, and journeys through the oases of Draa and Tafilet. With an introduction by Winwood Reade. Portrait. Map. 8°. London, 1874 . . . . 13 . 1351

ROLAND Cashel. C. Lever. Sm. 8°. London, 1872 . . . . 4 . 421

ROME. CASTELAR, EMILIO. Old Rome and new Italy. (Recuerdos de Italia.) *Trans.* by Mrs. Arthur Arnold. Sm. 8°. New York, 1874 13 . 1270

CHANNING, W. E. Conversations in Rome: between an artist, a catholic, and a critic. 16°. Boston, 1847 . . . . 13 . 828

MURRAY, JOHN, *publisher*. A hand-book of Rome and its environs. Eleventh edition, carefully revised on the spot to the latest period. With a large plan of Rome, a map of the environs, &c. Sm. 8°. London, 1873. . . . . 13 . 1176

SEYMOUR, M. H. A pilgrimage to Rome: containing some account of the high ceremonies, the monastic institutions, the religious services, the sacred relics, the miraculous pictures, and the general state of religion in that city. Illustrations. 4°. London, 1848 . . . . 13 . 1347

WITHROW, W. H. The catacombs of Rome, and their testimony relative to primitive Christianity. Illustrations. Sm. 8°. New York, 1874 . . . . 13 . 1141

ROOKWOOD. W. H. Ainsworth. 16°. London [n. d.] . . . . 4 . 1178

ROOSEVELT, Robert B. Progressive petticoats; or, dressed to death. An autobiography of a married man. 12°. New York, 1874 . . . . . 4 . 470

ROSA Lambert. G. W. M. Reynolds. 8°. Philadelphia [n. d.] . . . . . 4 . 544

ROSALIE'S pet. Joanna H. Mathews. (Juvenile.) 16°. New York, 1875. 4 . 377

*ROSE Foster. G. W. M. Reynolds. 8°. Philadelphia [n. d.] . . . . . . 4 . 540

ROSE Mather. M. J. Holmes. 12°. New York, 1874. 2 copies . . . . 3 . 1361–62

ROSE (A) in June. M. O. W. Oliphant. 8°. Boston, 1874 . . . . . . 4 . 525

ROSSEL, L. Nathaniel. Posthumous papers. Trans. from the French. 8°. London, 1872. . . . . 13 . 119

ROSSETTI, Christina G. Speaking likenesses. (Juvenile.) Illustrated. Sq. 16°. Boston, 1875 . . . . 4 . 452

ROSSETTI, William Michael. Memoir of William Blake. 16°. Boston, 1875 . . . . 21 . 248

ROUGH and ready. H. Alger, jun. 16°. Boston, 1869 . . . . 4 . 1158

ROWING and training, The arts of. With an appendix containing the laws of boat-racing, &c. By "Argonaut" (*pseud.*). Sm. 8°. London, 1866. 13 . 139

RUBY'S husband. M. V. Terhune. 12°. New York, 1873 . . . . 4 . 1115

RUFUS and Rose. H. Alger, jun. 16°. Boston, 1870 . . . . 4 . 1160

RULE, William H. History of the Inquisition from its establishment in the 12th century to its extinction in the 19th. Illustrations. 2 v. 8°. New York, 1874 . . . . 13 . 1062–63

RUNNING to waste. The story of a tomboy. G. M. Baker. 16°. Boston, 1875 . . . . 4 . 579
RUSLING, James F. Across America; or, the great West and the Pacific coast. Illustrated. Folded map. 12°. New York, 1874 . . . . . 13 . 134
RUSSIANS (The) in Central Asia. F. von Hellwald. Sm. 8°. London, 1874 . . . . .13 . 1235
RUSSIA'S advance eastward. Hugo Stumm. With an account of the Russian army by C. E. Howard Vincent. Sm. 8°. London, 1874 . . . 13 . 858
RYE-HOUSE (The) plot. G. W. M. Reynolds. 8°. Philadelphia [n. d.] . 4 . 545

S.

SABBATH, History of. J. M. Andrews. 12°. Battle Creek, Mich., 1873 . 13 . 1271
SABBATH school index. R. G. Pardee. 16°. Philadelphia, 1868 . . . 13 . 875
SABINA. *Lady* Wood. 16°. London, 1869. 2 copies . . . . 4 . 847–48
SACRED (The) anthology. M. D. Conway. 8°. New York, 1874 . . . 13 . 1068
SAILOR (The) boy. W. T. Adams. 16°. Boston, 1875 . . . . 4 . 305
SAINT James. W. H. Ainsworth. 16°. London [n. d.]. . . . . 4 . 1179
ST. Nicholas. Scribner's illustrated magazine for girls and boys. Vol. 1. 8°. New York, 1874 . . . . 12 . 301
ST. Ronan's well. *Sir* W. Scott. 2 v. in 1. 12°. Boston, 1874 . . . 4 . 232
SALEM. D. R. Castleton. 16°. New York, 1874 . . . . 4 . 267
SANDS, B. F. Report on observations of the total eclipse of the sun, Aug. 7, 1869. 4°. Washington, 1870 . . . . 11 . 752
SAND, George [*Pseud.*]. *See* DUDEVANT, A. L. A. D.
SATANSTOE. J. F. Cooper. 12°. New York, 1873 . . . . 4 . 1063
SAUZADE, John S. Mark Gildersleeve. (A novel.) 12°. New York, 1873. 4 . 1138
SAVGE, Minot Judson. Christianity the science of manhood: a book for questioners. 16°. Boston, 1875. . . . . 13 . 1147
*SAXE, *Count* Maurice de. Reveries or memoirs upon the art of war. To which are added some original letters upon various military subjects, wrote by the Count to the late King of Poland, and M. de Folard, which were never before made publick; with his reflections on the propagation of the human species. Trans. from the French. 4°. London, 1757 . . . . 13 . 1527
SCALP-HUNTERS (The). M. Reid. 12°. New York, 1874 . . . . 4 . 1260
SCEPTRES and crowns. S. Warner. 16°. New York, 1875 . . . . . . 4 . 376
SCHAFF, *Rev.* Philip, and PRIME, Samuel Irenæus (*editors*). Evangelical alliance conference, 1873. History, essays, orations, and other documents of the sixth general conference of the evangelical alliance, held in New York Oct. 2–12, 1873. L. 8°. New York, 1874 . . . . . 13 . 1301
SCHOOLS and schoolmasters. From the writings of Charles Dickens. Ed. by J. T. Chapman. 12°. New York, 1871 . . . . 4 . 1333
SCHOOLS for the people. George C. T. Bartley. 8°. London, 1871 . . 13 . 1418
SCHWEINFURTH, Georg A. The heart of Africa. Three years' travels in the unexplored regions of Central Africa from 1868 to 1871. Trans. by Ellen E. Frewer, with an introduction by Winwood Reade; with maps and woodcut-illustrations. 2 v. Roy. 8°. New York, 1874. 13 . 1311–12
SCIENCE (The) of sensibility. J. N. Smith. 16°. Philadelphia, 1875 . 13 . 1164

SCIENCE in story. E. B. Foote. 4 v. Sq. 8°. New York, 1874 . . 4 . 884–87
*SCIENTIFIC American. Vols. 12 to 31, inclusive. Folio. New York, 1865–74 . . . . 12 . 712–31
SCINTILLATIONS from the prose works of Heinrich Heine. Trans. from the German by S. A. Adler. 16°. New York, 1873 . . . . 4 . 867
SCOTT, *Sir* Walter. Waverley novels. Illustrated library edition. 25 vols.
Abbot (The). 2 v. in 1. 12°. Boston, 1874 . . . . 4 . 212
Anne of Geierstein. 2 v. in 1. 12°. Boston, 1873 . . . . 4 . 213
Antiquary (The). 2 v. in 1. 12°. Boston, 1873 . . . . 4 . 214
Betrothed (The), and The highland widow. 2 v. in 1. 12°. Boston, 1874 . . . . 4 . 215
Black dwarf, and A legend of Montrose. 2 v. in 1. 12°. Boston, 1873. 4 . 216
Bride of Lammermoor. 2 v. in 1. 12°. Boston, 1873 . . . . . . 4 . 217
Count Robert of Paris. 2 v. in 1. 12°. Boston, 1869 . . . . . . 4 . 218
Fair (The) maid of Perth. 2 v. in 1. 12°. Boston, 1874 . . . . 4 . 219
Fortunes (The) of Nigel. 2 v. in 1. 12°. Boston, 1872 . . . . . . 4 . 220
Guy Mannering. 2 v. in 1. 12°. Boston, 1874 . . . . 4 . 221
Heart (The) of Mid-Lothian. 2 v. in 1. 12°. Boston, 1874 . . . 4 . 222
Ivanhoe. 2 v. in 1. 12°. Boston, 1874 . . . . 4 . 223
Kenilworth. 2 v. in 1. 12°. Boston, 1874 . . . . 4 . 224
Monastery (The). 2 v. in 1. 12°. Boston, 1873 . . . . 4 . 225
Old Mortality. 2 v. in 1. 12°. Boston, 1873 . . . . 4 . 226
Peveril of the peak. 2 v. in 1. 12°. Boston, 1874 . . . . 4 . 227
Pirate (The). 2 v. in 1. 12°. Boston, 1873 . . . . 4 . 228
Quentin Durward. 2 v. in 1. 12°. Boston, 1868 . . . . 4 . 229
Redgauntlet. 2 v. in 1. 12°. Boston, 1872 . . . . 4 . 230
Rob Roy. 2 v. in 1. 12°. Boston, 1874 . . . . 4 . 231
St. Ronan's well. 2 v. in 1. 12°. Boston, 1874 . . . . 4 . 232
Surgeon's (The) daughter. Castle Dangerous. And index and glossary. 2 v. in 1. 12°. Boston, 1869 . . . . 4 . 233
Talisman (The). The two drovers; My aunt Margaret's mirror; The tapestried chamber; The Laird's Jock. 2 v. in 1. 12°. Boston, 1873. 4 . 234
Waverley. 2 v. in 1. 12°. Boston, 1874 . . . . 4 . 235
Woodstock. 2 v. in 1. 12°. Boston, 1872 . . . . 4 . 236
SCOTT, William B. Half-hour lectures on the history and practice of the fine and ornamental arts. 50 illustrations. 16°. New York, 1875. 13 . 1170
SCOTTISH anecdote, The book of. Ed. by A. Hislop. 8°. Edinburgh, 1874. 4 . 974
SCOTTISH (The) philosophy. J. McCosh. 8°. New York, 1875 . . . 13 . 1422
SCOTTISH rivers. *Sir* T. D. Lauder. Sm. 8°. Edinburgh, 1874 . . . 13 . 147
*SCULPTURE. Brigham, W. T. Cast catalogue of antique sculpture. 4°. Boston, 1874 . . . . 13 . 1510
SEA and shore. W. T. Adams. 16°. Boston, 1875 . . . . 4 . 331
SEA (The) and its living wonders. *Dr.* G. Hartwig. 8°. London, 1873 . 13 . 1318
SEA-LIONS (The). J. F. Cooper. 12°. New York, 1873 . . . . 4 . 1064
SECOND (The) wife. E. John. 12°. Philadelphia, 1874 . . . . 4 . 1142
SEEBOHM, Frederic. The era of the protestant revolution. With numerous maps. 16°. New York, 1874 . . . . 13 . 872
SEEK and find. W. T. Adams. 16°. Boston, 1875 . . . . 4 . 323
SEILER, *Madam* Emma. The voice in speaking. Trans. from the German by W. H. Furness. 16°. Philadelphia, 1875 . . . . 13 . 1165

SELF-CULTURE. J. S. Blackie. 16°. New York, 1874 . . . . 13 . 866
SELF-MADE woman; or, Mary Idyl's trials and triumphs. E. M. Buckingham. 12°. New York, 1873 . . . . 4 . 977
*SENECA, Lucius Annæus. Epistles with large annotations, wherein particularly the tenets of the antient philosophers are contrasted with the Divine precepts of the gospel. Trans. by Thomas Morell. 2 v. in 1. 4°. London, 1786. . . . . 13 . 1509
*SETHOS, Life of. John Terrasson. 2 v. 8°. London, 1732 . . . 13 . 841–42
SEVEN (The) ages of a village pauper. G. C. T. Bartley. Sm. 8°. London, 1874 . . . . 13 . 1167
SEVEN historic ages. A. Gilman. 16°. New York, 1874 . . . . 13 . 975
*SEWARD, William. Anecdotes of distinguished persons, chiefly of the present and two preceding centuries. Portraits and plates. 4 v. Sm. 8°. London, 1798 . . . . 13 . 1201–4
SEX and education. Ed. by *Mrs.* Julia Ward Howe. 16°. Boston, 1874. 13 . 863
SEX in education. E. H. Clarke. 16°. Boston, 1874 . . . . 13 . 862
SEYMOUR, *Rev.* M. Hobart. A pilgrimage to Rome. 4°. London, 1848 . 13 . 1347
SHAKSPEARE, and the emblem writers. H. Green. Roy. 8°. London, 1870 . . . . 21 . 205
SHAKSPEARE, Essays on. Karl Elze. 8°. London, 1874 . . . . 13 . 1320
SHAKSPEARE's poems, A concordance to. H. K. Furness. Roy. 8°. Philadelphia, 1874 . . . . 21 . 204
SHAMROCK and thistle. W. T. Adams. 16°. Boston, 1875 . . . . . . 4 . 344
SHE loved him madly. Gontran Borys. Trans. by O. Vibeur. 12°. New York, 1874 . . . . 4 . 374
SHEPHERD, Henry E. The history of the English language from the Teutonic invasion of Britain to the close of the Georgian era. 16°. New York, 1874 . . . . 13 . 1158
SHERIDAN, R. B. Works, dramas, poems, translations, speeches, and unfinished sketches. Ed. by F. Stainforth. Sm. 8°. London, 1874 . 21 . 225
SHIFTING winds. R. M. Ballantyne. 16°. Philadelphia [n. d.] . . . . 4 . 1209
SHINN, Earl. [*Edward Strahan.*] The new Hyperion: from Paris to Marly by way of the Rhine. With over 300 illustrations, from designs by Gustave Doré and others. 8°. Philadelphia, 1875 . . . . 4 . 522

Note. — The illustrations in this book are borrowed from "Le chemin des ecoliers," par F. B. Saintine [*pseud.* of Joseph Xavier Boniface], Paris, 1861. The text is in a large measure drawn from the same source.

SHORT (A) history of the English people, from A. D. 449 to 1874. J. R. Green. Maps and tables. Sm. 8°. London, 1874 . . . . 13 . 1163
SIEBE, Henry. The conquest of the sea. A book about divers and diving. With illustrations. Sm. 8°. London, 1873 . . . . 13 . 967
SILENCE (The) and the voices of God. F. W. Farrar. Sm. 8°. London, 1874 . . . . 13 . 928
SIMPLETON (The) and The wandering heir. C. Reade. Sm. 8°. Boston, 1873 . . . . 4 . 1128
SINGERS and songs. A. P. Putnam. 8°. Boston, 1875 . . . . 21 . 213
SINK or swim. H. Alger, jun. 16°. Boston, 1870 . . . . 4 . 1148
SIR Brook Fosbrooke. C. Lever. Sm. 8°. London, 1873 . . . . 4 . 422
SIR Jasper Carew. C. Lever. Sm. 8°. London, 1873 . . . . 4 . 423

SIX weeks in the saddle. S. E. Waller. Sm. 8°. London, 1874 . . . 13 . 121

SKEAT, Walter W. Specimens of English literature, from the "Ploughmans crede" to the "Shepheardes calender," A.D. 1394–A.D. 1579. With introduction, notes, and glossarial index. Sm. 8°. Oxford, 1871 . . . . 13 . 961

SKETCHES by Boz. C. Dickens. 12°. Boston [n. d.] . . . . 4 . 1330

SKETCHES in Italy and Greece. J. A. Symonds. Sm. 8°. London, 1874. 13 . 135

SLATER, Samuel. Memoir of. G. S. White. 8°. Philadelphia, 1836 . 13 . 1408

SLAVER's (A) adventures on land and sea. W. H. Thomes. 12°. Boston, 1875 . . . . 4 . 1135

SLAVONIC fairy tales. J. T Naaké. Sm. 8°. London, 1874 . . . . . . 4 . 1303

SLOW and sure. H. Alger, jun. 16°. Boston, 1872 . . . . 4 . 1164

SMILES, Samuel. The Huguenots in France after the revocation of the edict of Nantes: with a visit to the country of the Vaudois. Sm. 8°. New York, 1874. . . . . 13 . 1237

SMITH, H. David Lloyd's last will. 16°. New York [n. d.] . . . . . . 4 . 876

SMITH, John Nelson. The science of sensibility (Intelligence), or simple element of soul and the spirit of life and origin of species. 16°. Philadelphia, 1875 . . . . 13 . 1164

SMITH, Julie P. Ten old maids. A novel. 12°. New York, 1874. 2 copies . . . . 3 . 1369–70

*SMITHSONIAN cohtributionst o knowledge. 18 volumes. Vol. II. to XIX. inclusive. 4°. Washington, 1848–74 . . . . 11 . 1502–19

Vol. II. Agassiz, Louis. The classification of insects from embryological data. 1 plate.
Bailey, J. W. Microscopical examination of soundings made by the U. S. coast survey off the Atlantic coast of the U. S. 1 plate.
— Microscopical observations made in South Carolina, Georgia, and Florida. 3 plates.
Ellet, Charles. Contributions to the physical geography of the U. S. 1 plate.
Gibbes, Robert W. Mosasaurus and the three allied new genera, holcodus, conosaurus, and amphorosteus. 3 plates.
Hare, Robert. On the explosiveness of nitre, with a view to elucidate its agency in the tremendous explosion of July, 1845, in New York.
Lieber, Francis. On the vocal sounds of Laura Bridgman, the blind deaf-mute at Boston, compared with the elements of phonetic language. 1 plate.
Squier, E. G. Aboriginal monuments of the State of New York, comprising the results of original surveys and explorations; with an illustrative appendix. 14 plates.
Walker, Sears C. Researches relative to the planet Neptune.
Appendix: Downes, J. Occultations visible in the United States during the year 1851.
Walker, Sears C. Ephemeris of the planet Neptune for the date of the Lalande observations of May 8 and 10, 1795, and for the oppositions of 1846–51.

III. Davis, Charles H. The law of deposit of the flood tide: its dynamical action and office.
Girard, Charles. Contributions to the natural history of the fresh-water fishes of North America. 3 plates.
Gray, Asa. Plantæ Wrightianæ Texano-Neo-Mexicanæ. Part I. 10 plates.
Harvey, Wm. H. Nereis Boreali-Americana; or, contributions to a history of the marine algæ of North America. Part I. Melanospermeæ. 12 plates.
Locke, John. Observations on terrestrial magnetism.
Secchi, A. Researches on electrical rheometry. 3 plates.
Whittlesey, Charles. Description of ancient works in Ohio. 7 plates.
Appendix: Downes, J. Occultations visible in the U. S. and other parts of the world during the year 1852.
Walker, S. C. Ephemeris of the planet Neptune for the year 1852.

SMITHSONIAN contributions to knowledge (*continued*).

Vol. IV. Riggs, S. R. Grammar and dictionary of the Dakota language.
V. Gray, Asa. Plantæ Wrightianæ Texano-Neo-Mexicanæ. Part II. 4 plates.
Leidy, Joseph. A flora and fauna within living animals. 10 plates.
Memoir upon the extinct species of fossil ox. 5 plates.
Harvey, William H. Nereis Boreali-Americana. Part II. Rhodospermeæ. 24 plates.
Wyman, Jeffries. Anatomy of the nervous system of Rana Pipiens. 2 plates.
VI. Coffin, James H. On the winds of the northern hemisphere. 13 plates.
Leidy, Joseph. The ancient fauna of Nebraska; or, a description of remains of extinct mammalia and chelonia, from the Mauvaises Terres of Nebraska. 25 plates.
Torrey, John. Plantæ Fremontianæ; or, descriptions of plants collected by Col. J. C. Fremont in California. 10 plates.
Observations on the Batis Maritima of Linnæus. 1 plate.
On the Darlingtonia Californica, a new pitcher-plant from Northern California. 1 plate.
Stimdson, William. Synopsis of the marine invertebrata of Grand Manan, or the region round the bay of Fundy, New Brunswick. 3 plates.
Appendix: Downes, John. Occultations of planets and stars by the moon, during the year 1853.
VII. Bailey, J. W. Notes on new species and localities of microscopical organisms. 1 plate.
Chappelsmith, John. Account of a tornado near New Harmony, Ind., April 30, 1852. 1 map and 1 plate.
Lapham, I. A. The antiquities of Wisconsin. 55 plates.
Leidy, J. A memoir on the extinct sloth tribe of North America. 16 plates.
Appendix: Publications of learned societies, and periodicals, in the library of the Smithsonian Institution, Dec. 31, 1854. Part I.
VIII. Alvord, Benjamin. The tangencies of circles and of spheres. 9 plates.
Haven, Samuel F. Archæology of the United States; or, sketches historical and bibliographical of the progress of information and opinion respecting vestiges of antiquity in the U. S.
Jones, Joseph. Researches, chemical and physiological, concerning certain North American vertebrata. 27 wood-cuts.
Olmstead, D. On the recent secular period of the aurora borealis.
Appendix: Force, Peter. Record of auroral phenomena observed in the higher northern latitudes.
Publications of learned societies, and periodicals, in the library of the Smithsonian Institution. May, 1856. Part II.
. Gibbs, W., and Genth, F. A. Researches on the ammonia-cobalt bases.
Hitchcock, Edward. Illustrations of surface geology. 12 plates. Part I. On surface geology, especially that of the Connecticut Valley, in New England. Part II. On the erosions of the earth's surface, especially by rivers. Part III. Traces of ancient glaciers in Massachusetts and Vermont.
Mayer, Brantz. Observations on Mexican history and archæology, with a special notice of Zapotec remains as delineated in Mr. J. G. Sawkin's drawings of Malta. 4 plates.
Meech, L. W. On the relative intensity of the heat and light of the sun upon different latitudes of the earth. 6 plates.
Appendix: Runkle, John D. New tables for determining the values of the co-efficients in the perturbative functions of planetary motion, which depend upon the ratio of the mean distances.
Asteroid supplement to new tables for determining the values of $b^{(i)}_s$ and its derivatives.
X. Bowen, T. J. A grammar and dictionary of the Yoruba language, with an introductory description of the country and people of Yoruba. 1 map.
Harvey, W. H. Nereis Boreali-Americana. Part III. Chlorospermeæ. 14 plates.
Kane, E. K. Magnetical observations in the Arctic seas, made during the second Grinnell expedition in search of Sir John Franklin, in 1853, 1854, and 1855, at Van Rensselaer Harbor, and other points on the west coast of Greenland. Reduced and discussed by C. A. Schott. 1 plate.

SMITHSONIAN contributions to knowledge (*continued*).

Vol. XI. Bache, A. D. Discussion of the magnetic and meteorological observations made at the Girard College observatory, Philadelphia, in 1840–45. Part I.

Brewer, T. M. North American Oölogy. 5 plates.

Gilliss, J. M. An account of the total eclipse of the sun on Sept. 7, 1858, as observed near Olmos, Peru. 1 plate.

Kane, E. K. Meteorological observations in the Arctic seas, made during the second Grinnell expedition in search of Sir John Franklin, in 1853–55, at Van Rensselaer Harbor, and other points on the west coast of Greenland. Reduced and discussed by Charles A. Schott.

Le Conte, John L. The coleoptera of Kansas and eastern New Mexico. 3 plates.

Loomis, Elias. On certain storms in Europe and America, December, 1836. 13 plates.

Sonntag, August. Observations on terrestrial magnetism in Mexico. Conducted under the direction of Baron von Müller; with notes and illustrations of the volcano Popocatepetl and its vicinity. 1 plate.

XII. Caswell, Alexis. Meteorological observations made at Providence, R. I., extending over a period of twenty-eight years and a half, from December, 1831, to May, 1860.

Kane, E. K. Astronomical observations in the Arctic seas, made during the second Grinnell expedition in search of Sir John Franklin, in 1853–55, at Van Rensselaer Harbor, and other points in the vicinity of the north-west coast of Greenland. Reduced and discussed by S. C. Schott. 1 plate.

Mitchell, S. Weir. Researches upon the venom of the rattlesnake; with an investigation of the anatomy and physiology of the organs concerned. 12 wood-cuts.

Smith, N. D. Meteorological observations made near Washington, Ark., extending over a period of twenty years, from 1840 to 1859, inclusive.

Whittlesey, C. On fluctuations of level in the North American lakes. 2 plates.

XIII. Bache, A. D. Discussion of the magnetic and meteorological observations made at the Girard College Observatory, Philadelphia, in 1840–45. Part II. Investigation of the solar-diurnal variation of the magnetic declination, and its annual inequality. Part III. Investigation of the lunar effects on the magnetic declination. Parts IV., V., VI. Horizontal force. Investigation of the ten or eleven year period, and of the disturbances of the horizontal component of the magnetic force. Investigation of the solar-diurnal variation, and of the annual inequality of the horizontal force, and of the lunar effect on the same.

Records and results of a magnetic survey of Pennsylvania and parts of adjacent states in 1840–41, with some additional records and results of 1834–35, 1843, and 1862, and a map. 1 map.

Kane, E. K. Tidal observations in the Arctic seas, made during the second Grinnell expedition in search of Sir John Franklin, in 1853–55. Reduced and discussed by C. A. Schott. 4 plates.

McClintock, *Sir* Leopold. Meteorological observations in the Arctic seas, made on board the Arctic searching yacht "Fox," in Baffin Bay and Prince Regent Inlet, in 1857–59. Reduced and discussed by C. A. Schott. 1 map.

Mitchell, S. W., and Morehouse, G. R. Researches upon the anatomy and physiology of respiration in the chelonia.

Whittlesey, C. Ancient mining on the shores of Lake Superior. 1 map.

XIV. Bache, A. D. Discussion of the magnetic and meteorological observations made at the Girard College Observatory, Philadelphia, in 1840–45. Parts VII., VIII., and IX. Vertical force. Investigation of the eleven (or ten) year period, and of the disturbances of the vertical component of the magnetic force, and appendix on the magnetic effect of the aurora borealis; with an investigation of the solar-diurnal variation, and of the annual inequality of the vertical force; and of the lunar effect of the vertical force, the inclination, and total force. Parts X., XI., and XII. Dip and total force. Analysis of the disturbances of the dip and total force; discussion of the solar-diurnal variation and annual inequality of the dip and total force; and discussion of the absolute dip, with the final values for declination, dip, and force, between 1841 and 1845.

Draper, Henry. On the construction of a silvered glass telescope, fifteen and a half inches in aperture, and its use in celestial photography.

SMITHSONIAN contributions to knowledge. Vol. XIV. (*continued*).

Leidy, Joseph. Cretaceous reptiles of the United States. 20 plates.

Meek, F. B., and Hayden, F. V. Palæontology of the Upper Missouri. A report upon collections made principally by the expeditions under command of Lieut. G. K. Warren, U.S. Top. Eng'rs, in 1855-56. Invertebrates. Part I. 5 plates.

XV. Hayes, I. I. Physical observations in the Arctic seas, made on the west coast of North Greenland, the vicinity of Smith Strait, and the west side of Kennedy Channel, during 1860-61. 6 plates, and 14 wood-cuts.

Newcomb, Simon. An investigation of the orbit of Neptune, with general tables of its motion.

Pumpelly, Raphael. Geological researches in China, Mongolia, and Japan, during the years 1862-65. 9 plates, and 18 wood-cuts.

Whittlesey, C. On the fresh-water glacial drift of the northwestern states. 2 plates, and 11 wood-cuts.

XVI. Cleaveland, P. Results of meteorological observations made at Brunswick, Me., between 1807 and 1859. 8 wood-cuts.

Coffin, J. H. The orbit and phenomena of a meteoric fire-ball, seen July 20, 1860. 2 plates, and 2 wood-cuts.

Dean, John. The gray substance of the medulla oblongata and trapezium. 16 plates, and 5 wood-cuts.

Gould, B. A. On the transatlantic longitude.

Hildreth, S. P. Results of meteorological observations made at Marietta, O., between 1826 and 1859 inclusive; to which are added results of observations taken at Marietta, O., by Joseph Wood, between 1817 and 1823. 14 wood-cuts.

Pickering, C. On the Gliddon mummy case in the museum of the Smithsonian Institution. 1 plate.

Swan, J. G. The Indians of Cape Flattery, at the entrance to the strait of Fuca, Washington Territory. 44 wood-cuts.

XVII. Morgan, Lewis H. Systems of consanguinity and affinity of the human family. 14 plates, and 6 diagrams.

XVIII. Ferrel, William. Converging series expressing the ratio between the diameter and the circumference of a circle.

Harkness, William. Observations on terrestrial magnetism, and on the deviations of the compasses of the U.S. iron-clad "Monadnock," during her cruise from Philadelphia to San Francisco, in 1865 and 1866. 2 diagrams.

Henry, J. Tables and results of the precipitation, in rain and snow, in the United States; and at some stations in adjacent parts of North America, and in Central and South America. 8 diagrams, 5 plates, and 3 charts.

Stockwell, John N. Memoir on the secular variations of the elements of the orbits of the eight principal planets, Mercury, Venus, the Earth, Mars, Jupiter, Saturn, Uranus, and Neptune; with tables of the same. Together with the obliquity of the ecliptic, and the precession of the equinoxes in both longitude and right ascension.

XIX. Barnard, J. G. Problems of rotary motion presented by the gyroscope, the precession of the equinoxes, and the pendulum.

Newcomb, S. An investigation of the orbit of Uranus, with general tables of its motion.

Wood, H. C. A contribution to the history of the fresh-water algæ of North America. 21 colored plates.

Note. — This collection of works has been recently presented to the Library by the Smithsonian Institute, and is complete with the exception of Vol. I. which is out of print.

SMITHSONIAN institution. Annual reports of the regents, 1871-72. 2 v. 8°. Washington, 1873 . . . . 11 . 447-48

SOCIAL fetters. *Mrs.* Edwin James. Sm. 8°. London, 1869 . . . . 4 . 564

SOLDIER (The) boy. W. T. Adams. 16°. Boston, 1875 . . . . 4 . 302

* SOLDIERS' national cemetery at Gettysburg. J. R. Bartlett. 4°. Providence, 1874 . . . . 13 . 1506

SOME women's hearts. Louise C. Moulton. 16°. Boston, 1874 . . . . 4 . 372

SOMERVILLE, Martha. Personal recollections from early life to old age of Mary Somerville. With selections from her correspondence. 8°. Boston, 1874. . . . . 13 . 1257

SONGS of many seasons. 1862–1874. O. W. Holmes. 16°. Boston, 1875. . . . . 21 . 245
SOPHISMS of protection. F. Bastiat. 12°. New York, 1874 . . . . . . 13 . 942
SOPHOMORES (The) of Radcliffe. E. Kellogg. 16°. Boston, 1875 . . . 4 . 954
SORDELLO, a poem. Robert Browning. 16°. London, 1840 . . . . . . 21 . 236
* SOUTH America. Travels in South America. Paul Marcoy. 2 v. 4°. New York, 1875 . . . . 13 . 1507–8
SOUTH-SEA idyls. C. W. Stoddard. Sq. 16°. Boston, 1873 . . . . . . 13 . 886
SOUTHWORTH, Emma Dorothy Eliza Nevitte. Allworth abbey. 12°. Philadelphia, 1865 . . . . 4 . 1001
The artist's love. And stories by *Mrs.* Frances Henshaw Baden. 12°. Philadelphia, 1872. . . . . 4 . 1002
A beautiful fiend; or, through the fire. 12°. Philadelphia, 1873. 2 copies . . . . 4 . 1003–4
Victor's triumph. *Sequel* to "A beautiful fiend." 12°. Philadelphia, 1874 . . . . 4 . 1005
The bridal eve. 12°. Philadelphia, 1864 . . . . 4 . 1006
The bride of Llewellyn. 12°. Philadelphia, 1866 . . . . 4 . 1007
The changed brides. 12°. Philadelphia, 1869 . . . . 4 . 1008
The bride's fate. *Sequel* to "The changed brides." 12°. Philadelphia, 1869 . . . . 4 . 1009
Cruel as the grave. 12°. Philadelphia, 1871 . . . . 4 . 1010
Tried for her life. *Sequel* to "Cruel as the grave." 12°. Philadelphia, 1871 . . . . 4 . 1011
The curse of Clifton. 12°. Philadelphia, 1874 . . . . 4 . 1012
The deserted wife. 12°. Philadelphia, 1855 . . . . 4 . 0113
The discarded daughter. 12°. Philadelphia, 1852 . . . . 4 . 1014
Fair play; or, the test of the lone isle. 12°. Philadelphia, 1868 . . 4 . 1015
How he won her. *Sequel* to "Fair play." 12°. Philadelphia, 1869. 4 . 1016
Fallen pride; or, the mountain girl's love. 12°. Philadelphia, 1868. 4 . 1017

Note. — This work is the same as that published under the title "The curse of Clifton."

The family doom; or, the sin of a countess. 12°. Philadelphia, 1869. 4 . 1018
The maiden widow. *Sequel* to "The family doom." 12°. Philadelphia, 1870 . . . . 4 . 1019
The fatal marriage. 12°. Philadelphia, 1863 . . . . 4 . 1020
The fortune seeker. 12°. Philadelphia, 1866 . . . . 4 . 1021
The gypsy's prophecy; or the bride of an evening. 12°. Philadelphia, 1861 . . . . 4 . 1022
The haunted homestead, and other novellettes; with an autobiography of the author. 12°. Philadelphia, 1860 . . . . 4 . 1023
India: the pearl of Pearl river. 12°. Philadelphia, 1857 . . . . . . 4 . 1024
The lady of the isle. A romance from real life. 12°. Philadelphia, 1857 . . . . 4 . 1025
The lost heir of Linlithgow. 12°. Philadelphia, 1872 . . . . 4 . 1026
A noble lord. *Sequel* to "The lost heir of Linlithgow." 12°. Philadelphia, 1872 . . . . 4 . 1027
The lost heiress. 12°. Philadelphia, 1854 . . . . 4 . 1028
Love's labor won. 12°. Philadelphia, 1862 . . . . 4 . 1029

SOUTHWORTH, Emma Dorothy Eliza Nevitte (*continued*).
Miriam the avenger; or, the missing bride. Portrait of the author. 12°. Philadelphia, 1874 . . . . 4 . 1030
The mother-in-law. A tale of domestic life. 12°. Philadelphia, 1860 4 . 1031
The prince of darkness. 12°. Philadelphia, 1869 . . . . 4 . 1032
Retribution. 12°. Philadelphia, 1856 . . . . 4 . 1033
The three beauties. 12°. Philadelphia, 1858 . . . . 4 . 1034
The two sisters. 12°. Philadelphia, 1858 . . . . 4 . 1035
Vivia; or, the secret of power. 12°. Philadelphia, 1857 . . . . . . 4 . 1036
The widow's son. 12°. Philadelphia, 1867 . . . . 4 . 1037
The wife's victory; and other novellettes. 12°. Philadelphia, 1854 . 4 . 1038
And BADEN, Frances Henshaw. The Christmas guest. 12°. Philadelphia, 1870 . . . . 4 . 1039
SOWED by the wind. E. Kellogg. 16°. Boston, 1875 . . . . 4 . 946
SPARK (The) of genius. E. Kellogg. 16°. Boston, 1875 . . . . 4 . 953
SPEAKING likenesses. C. G. Rossetti. (Juvenile.) Sq. 16°. Boston, 1875 . . . . 4 . 452
SPECIMENS of English literature. 1394–1579. W. W. Skeat. Sm. 8°. Oxford, 1871 . . . . 13 . 961
SPENDTHRIFT (The). W. H. Ainsworth. 16°. London [n. d.] . . . 4 . 1180
SPICER, Henry. Judicial dramas; or, the romance of French criminal law. 8°. London, 1872 . . . . .13 . 1218
SPORTSMAN'S (The) club afloat. C. A. Fosdick. 16°. Cincinnati, 1874 . 4 . 972
SPORTSMAN'S (The) club among the trappers. C. A. Fosdick. 16°. Cincinnati, 1874. . . . . 4 . 973
SPORTSMAN'S (The) club in the saddle. C. A. Fosdick. 16°. Cincinnati, 1873 . . . . 4 . 974
SPRING floods; and A Lear of the steppe. Ivan S. Turgénieff. 16°. New York, 1874 . . . . 4 . 873
SPURGEON, C. H. Flashes of thought; being one thousand choice extracts from his works. Alphabetically arranged, and with a copious index. Sm. 8°. London, 1874 . . . . 13 . 126
SPY (The). J. F. Cooper. 12°. New York, 1874 . . . . 4 . 1065
STABLES, W. Gordon. "Cats:" their points and characteristics, with curiosities of cat life, and a chapter on feline ailments. Colored plates. Sm. 8°. London [n. d.] . . . . 13 . 176
STANLEY, Henry M. Coomassie and Magdala: the story of two British campaigns in Africa. Illustrations. 2 maps. 8°. New York, 1874. 13 . 1309
STAR-CHAMBER (The). W. H. Ainsworth. 16°. London [n. d] . . . . 4 . 1181
STARLING (The). N. Macleod. 16°. New York [n. d.] . . . . 4 . 1137
STARRY (The) flag. W. T. Adams. 16°. Boston, 1875. . . . . 4 . 320
STEFFENS, Heinrich. German university life. Trans. by W. L. Gage. 12°. Philadelphia, 1874 . . . . .13 . 1161
STEINMETZ, Andrew. The gaming table: its votaries and victims in all times and countries, especially in England and France. 2 v. 8°. London, 1870 . . . . 13 . 1054–55
STEPHENS, Ann S. Phemie's Frost's experiences. 12°. New York, 1874. 4 . 357
STEPHENS, Charles Asbury. The young moose hunters; a backwoods-boy's story. Illustrated. Sm. 8°. Boston, 1874. 2 copies . . . . 4 . 909–10
STERLING, John. Life of. T. Carlyle. 16°. New York, 1871 . . . . 13 . 867

STEWART, Balfour. The conservation of energy. With an appendix treating of the vital and mental applications of the doctrine. Sm. 8°. New York, 1874 . . . . 13 . 136
STILLMAN, William J. The Cretan insurrection of 1866–68. 8°. New York, 1874 . . . . 13 . 137
STOCKTON, Frank R. What might have been expected. Illustrated. 16°. New York, 1874 . . . . 4 . 842
STODDARD, Charles Warren. South-sea idyls. Sq. 16°. Boston, 1873 . 13 . 886
STODDARD, Richard Henry, *editor*. Bric-a-brac series. Personal reminiscences by Chorley, Planché, and Young. Sq. 16°. New York, 1874. 13 . 970
Anecdote biographies of Thackeray and Dickens. Sq. 16°. New York, 1874 . . . . 13 . 971
Prosper Méremee's letters to an incognita, with recollections by Lamartine and George Sand. Sq. 16°. New York, 1874 . . 13 . 972
Personal reminiscences by Barham, Harness, and Hodder. Sq. 16°. New York, 1875 . . . . 13 . 973
The Greville memoirs: a journal of the reigns of King George IV. and King William IV, by Charles C. F. Greville. Sq. 16°. New York, 1875 . . . . 13 . 974
STODDARD, William Osborn. Verses of many days. 16°. New York, 1875. 21 . 231
STORIES and tales. H. C. Andersen. 12°. New York, 1872 . . . . . 4 . 253
STORIES of animal sagacity. W. H. G. Kingston. Sm. 8°. London, 1874. 4 . 933
STORIES of the Peninsular war. W. H. Maxwell. Sm. 8°. London [n. d.] 4 . 432
STORIES of Waterloo. W. H. Maxwell. Sm. 8°. London [n. d.] . . . 4 . 433
STORIES (The) they tell me; or, Sue and I. E. G. O'Reilly. 16°. New York, 1874 . . . . 4 . 480
STORM warriors; or, life-boat work. John Gilmore. Sm. 8°. London, 1874 . . . . 13 . 120
STORY (The) of a house. E. E. Viollet-Leduc. 8°. Boston, 1874 . . . 4 . 1301
STORY (The) of a summer. C. Cleveland. Sq. 16°. New York, 1874 . 4 . 883
STORY (The) of a cummer day. (Juvenile.) By the author of "Busy bee," &c. With illustrations. Sm. 4°. New York [n. d.] . . . 4 . 1302
STOUT (A) heart. E. Kellogg. 16°. Boston, 1875 . . . . 4 . 958
STOWE, Harriet (Elizabeth) Beecher. Nina Gordon: a tale of the Great Dismal Swamp. 2 v. in 1. 12°. Boston, 1874 . . . . 4 . 355
STRAHAN, Edward [*Pseud.*]. *See* SHINN, Earl.
STRANGE (The) adventures of a phaeton. W. Black. Sm. 8°. London, 1874 . . . . 4 . 265
STRENGTH and beauty. M. Hopkins. 16°. New York, 1874 . . . . . 13 . 1166
STRIVE and succeed. H. Alger, jun. 16°. Boston, 1872 . . . . 4 . 1150
STRIVELYNE, Elsie [*Pseud.*]. The princess of Silverland, and other tales. (Juvenile.) With a frontispiece by *Sir* Noel Paton. Sm. 8°. London, 1874 . . . . 4 . 832
STRONG and steady. H. Alger, jun. 16°. Boston, 1871 . . . . 4 . 1149
STUMM, Hugo. Russia's advance eastward, with other information on the subject, and an account of the Russian army, by C. E. Howard Vincent. Map. Sm. 8°. London, 1874 . . . . 13 . 858
SUB-TROPICAL (The) garden. W. Robinson. Sm. 8°. London, 1871 . . 13 . 113
SUMNER, Charles. Life and public services. C. E. Lester. L. 8°. New York, 1874 . . . . 13 . 1314

SUMNER, Charles (*continued*).
*Memorial. 4°. Boston, 1874 . . . . 13 . 1530
Prophetic voices concerning America. 8°. Boston, 1874 . . . . . . 13 . 1251
Works. Vols. 8, 9. 8°. Boston, 1873–4 . . . . 13 . 1246–47

SUMNER, William Graham. History of American currency. With chapters on English bank restriction and Austrian paper money, to which is appended "The Bullion Report." 12°. New York, 1874 . . . 13 . 933

SUNNYBANK. M. V. Terhune. 12°. New York, 1874 . . . .

SUNNY shores. W. T. Adams. 16°. Boston, 1875 . . . . 4 . 352

SUPERHUMAN (The) origin of the Bible. H. Rogers. Sm. 8°. New York, 4 . 1116
1874 . . . . 13 . 1354

SUPERSTITIONS of medicine and surgery. T. J. Pettigrew. 8°. London, 1844 . . . . 13 . 1234

SURGEON'S (The) daughter; Castle Dangerous. *Sir* W. Scott. 2 v. in 1. 12°. Boston, 1869 . . . . 4 . 233

* SWAMMERDAM, John. The book of nature; or, the history of insects reduced to distinct classes, confirmed by particular instances displayed in the anatomical analysis of many species, and illustrated with copper plates. With the life of the author by Herman Boerhaave, M.D. Trans. from the Dutch and Latin original edition by Thomas Flloyd. Revised and improved by notes from Reaumur and others, by John Hill, M.D. Folio. London, 1758 . . . . 15 . 1415

SWINBURNE, Algernon Charles. Bothwell: a tragedy. Sm. 8°. London, 1874 . . . . 21 . 222

Note. — This work is founded upon events in the lives of Mary Queen of Scots and her husband, James Hepburn, earl of Bothwell.

SWING, David. Truths for to-day, spoken in the past winter. 16°. Chicago, 1874 . . . . 13 . 927

Note. — This work contains a declaration from Mr. Swing, in reply to the charges of Prof. Patton.

SWINTON, William. Outlines of the world's history, ancient, mediæval, and modern, with special relation to the history of civilization and the progress of mankind. Illustrations and Maps. Sm. 8°. New York, 1874 . . . . 13 . 1177

SWISS allmends, and a walk to see them. F. B. Zincke. Sm. 8°. London, 1874. (*See* ZINCKE, Foster Barham) . . . . 13 . 953

SWITCH off. W. T. Adams. 16°. Boston, 1875 . . . . 4 . 317

*SYMBOLORUM et emblematum ex re herbaria desumtorum centuria una. Joachimo Camerario. 4°. Norimberg, 1590 . . . . 13 . 914

SYMINGTON, Maggie. Working to win: a story for girls. 12°. New York [n. d.] . . . . 4 . 469

SYMONDS, John A. Sketches in Italy and Greece. Sm. 8°. London, 1874 13 . 135

SYRIAN home-life. *Rev.* Henry H. Jessup. 16°. New York, 1874 . . . 13 . 124

T.

TAINE, Hippolyte Adolphe. History of English literature. Trans. by H. Van Laun. 4 v. 8°. Edinburgh, 1873 . . . . 13 . 1210–13
A Tour through the Pyrenees. 12°. New York, 1874 . . . . 13 . 1260

TAKE a peep. Paul Cobden [*Pseud.*]. 16°. Boston, 1874 . . . . . . 4 . 438
TALE (A) of two cities. C. Dickens. 12°. Boston, 1874 . . . . 4 . 1331
TALES of the feudal period. Ed. by Wm. Carew Hazlitt. Sm. 8°. London 1873 . . . . 4 . 833
TALS of old travel re-narrated. H. Kingsley. Sm. 8. London, 1870 . . 4 . 465
TALISMAN (The). The two drovers; My aunt Margaret's mirror; The tapestried chamber; The Laird's Jock. *Sir* W. Scott. 2 v. in 1. 12°. Boston, 1873 . . . . 4 . 234
TANNAHILL, Robert, and WILSON, John. Poetical works with lives. 2 v. in 1. 12°. London, 1851 . . . . 21 . 235
TATTERED TOM. H. Alger, jun. 16°. Boston, 1871 . . . . 4 . 1161
TAYLOR, Benjamin F. Old-time pictures, and sheaves of rhyme. Illustrated. Sq. 16°. Chicago, 1875 . . . . 21 . 232
The world on wheels, and other sketches. Sm. 8°. Chicago, 1874 . . 4 . 262
TAYLOR, Isaac. *The third.* Etruscan researches. Illustrated. 8°. London, 1874 . . . . 13 . 1241
TAYLOR, (James) Bayard, *compiler.* Central Asia. Travels in Cashmere, Little Tibet, and Central Asia. Illustrated. 12°. New York, 1874. 13 . 945
Egypt and Iceland in the year 1874. 12°. New York, 1874 . . . . 13 . 946
TAYLOR, Joseph. A fast life on the modern highway; being a glance into the railroad world from a new point of view. Illustrated. 12°. New York, 1874 . . . . 4 . 261
TAYLOR, Tom. Leicester square; its associations and its worthies. With a sketch of Hunter's scientific character and works by Richard Owen, with illustrations. Sm. 8°. London, 1874 . . . . 13 . 947
TAYLOR, William M. David, king of Israel; his life and its lessons. 8°. New York, 1875 . . . . 13 . 1125
TECHNICAL training. T. Twining. 8°. London, 1874. . . . . 13 . 1321
TEMPEST and sunshine. M. J. Holmes. 12°. New York, 1874. 2 copies. 3 . 1363–64
TEMPEST-TOSSED. T. Tilton. 12°. New York, 1874. 2 copies . . . . 4 . 903–4
TEN days in Spain. Kate Field. Sq. 16°. Boston, 1875 . . . . 13 . 977
TEN-MINUTE talks on all sorts of topics. Elihu Burritt. 16°. Boston, 1874. 13 . 959
TEN old maids. Julie P. Smith. 12°. New York, 1874. 2 copies . 3 . 1369–70
TEN thousand a year. S. Warren. 2 v. in 1. Sm. 8°. Edinburgh, 1873. 4 . 468
TERHUNE, Mary Virginia [*Marion Harland*], *formerly Miss Hawes.* Alone. 12°. New York, 1874 . . . . 4 . 1101
At last. 12°. New York, 1874. . . . . 4 . 1102
The empty heart; or, husks. 12°. New York, 1874 . . . . 4 . 1103
From my youth up. 12°. New York, 1874. 2 copies . . . . . . 4 . 1104–5
Helen Gardner's wedding-day; or, Col. Floyd's wards. 12°. New York, 1873. 2 copies . . . . 4 . 1106–7
The hidden path. 12°. New York, 1874 . . . . 4 . 1108
Husbands and homes. 12°. New York, 1874 . . . . 4 . 1109
Jessamine. 12°. New York, 1874. . . . . 4 . 1110
Miriam. 12°. New York, 1874 . . . . 4 . 1111
Moss-side. 12°. New York, 1874 . . . . 4 . 1112
Nemesis. 12°. New York, 1874 . . . . 4 . 1113
Phemie's temptation. 12°. New York, 1874 . . . . 4 . 1114
Ruby's husband. 12°. New York, 1873 . . . . 4 . 1115
Sunnybank. 12°. New York, 1874 . . . . 4 . 1116
True as steel. 12°. New York, 1874. . . . . 4 . 1117

*TERRASSON, John. The life of Sethos, taken from private memoirs of the ancient Egyptians. 2 v. 8°. London, 1732 . . . . 13 . 841–42
TERRIBLE (A) secret. M. A. Fleming. 12°. New York, 1874 . . . . . 4 . 1335
TERRIBLE (A) temptation. C. Reade. Sm. 8°. Boston, 1872 . . . . . 4 . 1129
TESTIMONY (The) of the evangelists. Simon Greenleaf. L. 8°. New York, 1874 . . . . 13 . 1307
THACKERAY and Dickens, Anecdote biographies of. Ed. by R. H. Stoddard. 16°. New York, 1874 . . . . 13 . 971
THAT boy of Norcott's. C. Lever. Sm. 8°. London, 1873 . . . . . . 4 . 424
THAT queer girl. V. F. Townsend. Sq. 16°. Boston, 1875 . . . . . . 4 . 368
THEOLOGY in the English poets. S. A. Brooke. Sm. 8°. New York, 1875. 13 . 1126
THEORY of the glaciers of Savoy. Louis Rendu. 8°. London, 1874 . . 13 . 1330
THOLUCK, Augustus. A translation and commentary of the book of Psalms. Trans. from the German, with a careful comparison of the Psalm text, by *Rev.* J. Isidor Mombert. 12°. Philadelphia, 1858 . 13 . 1238
THOMAS, Annie. *See* CUDLIP, Annie.
THOMES, William H. The gold-hunters' adventures; or, life in Australia. Illustrated. 12°. Boston, 1874 . . . . 4 . 1132
The bush-rangers: a Yankee's adventures during his second visit to Australia. Illustrated. 12°. Boston, 1875 . . . . 4 . 1132
The gold-hunters in Europe; or, the dead alive. Illustrated. 12°. Boston, 1874 . . . . 4 . 1133
Life in the East Indies. Illustrated. 12°. Boston, 1875 . . . . . . 4 . 1134
A slaver's adventures on land and sea. Illustrated. 12°. Boston, 1875 4 . 1153
The whaleman's adventures in the Sandwich islands and California. Illustrated. 12°. Boston, 1875 . . . . 4 . 1136
THOMPSON, Ella W. Beaten paths; or, a woman's vacation. 16°. Boston, 1874 . . . . 4 . 831
THOMS, William J. Human longevity, its facts and fictions. Sm. 8°. London, 1873 . . . . 13 . 844
THREE (The) beauties. E. D. E. N. Southworth. 12°. Philadelphia, 1858 . . . . 4 . 1034
THREE (The) homes: a tale for fathers and sons. F. T. L. Hope. 12°. New York, [n. d.] . . . . .4 . 462
THREE years in the federal cavalry. W. Glazier. Sm. 8°. New York, 1874 . . . . 13 . 1153
THREE years' slavery among the Patagonians. A. Guinnard. 8°. London, 1871 . . . . 13 . 143
THROUGH by daylight. W. T. Adams. 16°. Boston, 1875 . . . . . . 4 . 314
THROUGH thick and thin. J. Mery. 12°. New York, 1874 . . . . . . 4 . 474
THROWN together. F. Montgomery. 16°. New York, 1872 . . . . . . 4 . 472
TIGER-HUNTER (The). M. Reid. 12°. New York, 1874 . . . . 4 . 1261
TILTON, Theodore. Tempest-tossed. A romance. 12°. New York, 1874. 2 copies . . . . 4 . 903–4
TIROL, The valleys of. *Miss* R. H. Busk. Sm. 8°. London, 1874 . . . 13 . 936
TOM Bowling. W. James. 12°. London [n. d.] . . . . 4 . 437
TOM Burke of "ours." C. Lever. Sm. 8°. London, 1872 . . . . . 4 . 425
TOM Newcombe. C. A. Fosdick. 16°. Cincinnati, 1868 . . . . 4 . 959
TOOKE, William. Varieties of literature, from foreign literary journals and original MSS. 2 v. 8°. London, 1795 . . . . 13 . 1205–6

TOUR of James Monroe. S. Putnam Waldo. 16°. Hartford, 1818 . . 13 . 869
TOWER (The) of London. An historical romance. W. H. Ainsworth. 16°. London [n. d.] . . . . 4 . 1182
TOWNSEND, Luther Tracy. The arena and the throne. 1 colored plate. Sm. 8°. Boston, 1874 . . . . 13 . 1175
Lost forever. 16°. Boston, 1875 . . . . 4 . 369
TOWNSEND, Virginia Frances. That queer girl. Illustrated. Sq. 16°. Boston, 1875 . . . . 4 . 368
TRAFTON, Adeline. Katherine Earle. A novel. Illustrated. Sm. 8°. Boston, 1875 . . . . 4 . 354
TRAVELLER'S guide. *See* OSGOOD'S middle states.
TRAVELS in Central Asia, Cashmere, and Little Tibet. Ed. by Bayard Taylor. 12°. New York, 1874 . . . . 13 . 945
TRAVELS in Indo-China, Cambodia, and Laos. Henri Mouhot. 2 v. 8°. London, 1864. . . . . 13 . 1348–49
* TRAVELS in South America. Paul Marcoy. 2 v. 4°. New York, 1875. 13 . 1507–8
* TREATISE of the Epick poem. Rene le Bossu. 2 v. Sm. 8°. London, 1719 . . . . 13 . 881–82
TREATISE on the management of infancy. Andrew Combe, M.D. 12°. Philadelphia, 1842. 13 . 850
TRESPASSERS: showing how the inhabitants of earth, air, and water are enabled to trespass on domains not their own. J. G. Wood. Sq. 8°. New York [n. d.] . . . . 13 . 1133
TRIED for her life. E. D. E. N. Southworth. 12°. Philadelphia, 1871 . 4 . 1011
TROLLOPE, Anthony. Phineas Redux. 8°. New York, 1874 . . . . 4 . 528
TROLLOPE, T. Adolphus. Diamond cut diamond. A story of Tuscan life. 16°. New York, 1874 . . . . 4 . 466
TROPICAL (The) world. *Dr.* G. Hartwig. 8°. London, 1873 . . . . 13 . 1319
TROWBRIDGE, John Townsend. The emigrant's story, and other poems. 16°. Boston, 1875 . . . . 21 . 246
Fast friends. Illustrated. 16°. Boston, 1875. 2 copies . . . . . 4 . 574–5
Jack Hazard and his fortunes. Illustrated. 16°. Boston, 1873 . . 4 . 576
TRUE as steel. M. V. Terhune. 12°. New York, 1874. . . . . . . 4 . 1117
TRUE to him ever. Fannie W. Rankin. Sm. 8°. New York, 1874 . . 4 . 980
TRUST (The) and the remittance. Mary C. Clarke. 16°. Boston, 1874 21 . 238
TRUTHS for to-day. D. Swing. 16°. Chicago, 1874 . . . . 13 . 927
TRY again. W. T. Adams. 16°. Boston, 1875 . . . . 4 . 311
TRY and trust. H. Alger, jun. 16°. Boston, 1873 . . . . 4 . 1151
TURGÉNIEFF, Ivan S. Liza; or, a nest of nobles. Trans. from the Russian, by W. R. S. Ralston. 16°. New York, 1873 . . . . 4 . 871
On the eve. Trans. from the Russian, by C. E. Turner. 16°. New York, 1873 . . . . 4 . 872
Spring floods. Trans. from the Russian, by *Mrs.* Sophie Michell Butts. A Lear of the steppe. Trans. from the French, by W. H. Browne. 16°. New York, 1874 . . . . 4 . 873
TURNING (The) of the tide. E. Kellogg. 16°. Boston, 1875. . . . . 4 . 957
TWAIN, Mark [*Pseud.*]. *See* CLEMENS, S. L.
TWELVE miles from a lemon. M. A. Dodge. 16°. New York, 1874 . . 4 . 583
TWENTY thousand leagues under the seas. Jules Verne. 8°. Boston, 1875 . . . . 4 . 1234

TWINING, Thomas. Technical training; being a suggestive sketch of a national system of industrial instruction, founded on a general diffusion of practical science among the people. 8°. London, 1874 . . . . 13 . 1321
TWO (The) admirals. J. F. Cooper. 12°. New York, 1873 . . . . . . 4 . 1066
TWO (The) sisters. E. D. E. N. Southworth. 12°. Philadelphia, 1858 . 4 . 1035
TWO years in East Africa. E. Jonveaux. Sm. 8°. London, 1875 . . . 13 . 965
TYLOR, Edward B. Primitive culture; researches into the development of mythology, philosophy, religion, language, art, and custom. 2 v. 8°. Boston, 1874 . . . . 13 . 1065-66
TYNG, Stephen Higginson. The office and duty of a Christian pastor. Published at the request of the students and faculty of the school of theology in the Boston university. 16°. New York, 1874 . . . . 13 . 138

U.

UBIQUE [*Pseud.*]. *See* GILLMORE, Parker.
UGLY-GIRL papers. *Mrs.* S. D. Power. Sq. 16°. New York, 1875 . . 4 . 877
UNCOMMERCIAL traveller. C. Dickens. 12°. Boston, 1872 . . . . . . 4 . 1332
UNDER the evergreens. G. C. Lorimer. 16°. Boston, 1874 . . . . . . 4 . 834
UNDER the greenwood tree. T. Hardy. 16°. New York, 1874 . . . . 4 . 866
UNDER the trees. S. I. Prime. Sm. 8°. New York, 1874 . . . . . . 13 . 1243
UNDERWOOD, Francis Henry. Lord of himself. A novel. 12°. Boston, 1874 . . . . 4 . 934
UNITED States coast survey report, showing the progress of the survey during the year 1870. 4°. Washington, 1873 . . . . 11 . 751
UNITED States geological survey of a portion of the territories of Montana, Idaho, Wyoming, and Utah. F. V. Hayden. 8°. Washington, 1873 . 11 . 749
UNITED States geological survey of Nebraska and portions of the adjacent territories. F. V. Hayden. 8°. Washington, 1872 . . . . 11 . 750
UNITED States, History of. Vol. X. From 1778 to 1782. George Bancroft. 8°. Boston, 1874 . . . . 20 . 1228
UNITED States Report on the treatment of prisoners of war, by the rebel authorities, during the war of the rebellion; to which are appended the testimony taken by the committee, and official documents and statistics, &c. 8°. Washington, 1869 . . . . 11 . 748
UNWRITTEN history: life among the Modocs. J. Miller. 8°. Hartford, 1874 4 . 547
UP the Baltic. W. T. Adams. 16°. Boston, 1874 . . . . 4 . 349
UPTON, George P., *translator*. Memories: a story of German love. Sq. 16°. Chicago, 1875 . . . . 4 . 849
URBANE and his friends. E. Prentiss. 12°. New York, 1874 . . . . 4 . 557
URE, Andrew. Dictionary of arts, manufactures, and mines. Illustrated with nearly 1600 engravings on wood. 2 v. Roy. 8°. New York, 1853 . . . . 13 . 1403-4

V.

VALENTINE the countess; or, between father and son. Carl Detlef. 12°. Philadelphia, 1874 . . . . 4 . 259
VALERIE. F. Marryat. 12°. London [n. d.] . . . . 4 . 252
*VARIETIES of literature. W. Tooke. 2 v. 8°. London, 1795 . . 13 . 1205–6
*VENIETIA Trelawney. G. W. M. Reynolds. 8°. Philadelphia [n. d.] . 4 . 542
VERNE, Jules. Adventures in the land of the behemoth [Africa]. Illustrated. Sm. 8°. Boston, 1874. 2 copies . . . . 4 . 1212–13

Note. — Also published, with some variations, under the title of Meridiana.

Around the world in eighty days. Trans. by George M. Towle. Illustrated. Sq. 16°. Boston, 1874 . . . . 4 . 1214
Dr. Ox's experiment, and other stories. Trans. from the French. Illustrated. Sq. 16°. Boston, 1875. 2 copies . . . . 4 . 1215–16

Contents. — Dr. Ox's experiment; Master Zacharius; A drama in the air; A winter amid the ice; Ascent of Mont Blanc.

Five weeks in a balloon; or, journeys and discoveries in Africa by three Englishmen. Done into English by "William Lackland." 48 heliotype illustrations. Sm. 8°. Boston, 1874. 2 copies . . 4 . 1217–18
A floating city, and The blockade runners. Illustrated. Sq. 16°. New York, 1874 . . . . 4 . 1219
The same. Sq. 16°. New York, 1875 . . . . 4 . 1220
From the clouds to the mountains; comprising narratives of strange adventures by air, land, and water. With a chapter by Paul Verne. Trans. by A. L. Alger. Illustrated. Sq. 12°. Boston, 1874. 2 copies . . . . 4 . 1221–22

Contents. — A drama in mid-air; Dr. Ox's hobby; Master Zachary; A winter among the ice-fields; The fortieth French ascent of Mont Blanc.

From the earth to the moon, direct in ninety-seven hours and twenty minutes; and a trip around it. Illustrated. Trans. from the French by Louis Mercier, and Eleanor E. King. 8°. New York, 1874. 2 copies . . . . 4 . 1223–24
The fur country; or, seventy degrees north latitude. Trans. from the French by N. d'Anvers. 100 illustrations. 8°. Boston, 1874. 2 copies . . . . 4 . 1225–26
A journey to the centre of the earth. Illustrated. Sq. 16°. Boston [n. d.] 4 . 1227
A journey to the north pole. Illustrated. Sm. 8°. New York, 1875. 2 copies . . . . 4 . 1228 29
The field of ice. *A sequel* to A journey to the north pole. Illustrated. Sm. 8°. New York, 1875. 2 copies . . . . 4 . 1230–31
The mysterious island. Part first. Shipwrecked in the air. Trans. from the French. 42 illustrations. 12°. Boston, 1875. 2 copies. 4 . 1232–33
Twenty thousand leagues under the seas; or, the marvellous and exciting adventures of Pierre Arounax, Conseil his servant, and Ned Land, a Canadian harpooner. Trans. from the French. 110 illustrations. 8°. Boston, 1875 . . . . 4 . 1234

VERNE, Jules (*continued*).

A voyage round the world, in search of the castaways; a romantic narrative of the loss of Capt. Grant of the brig Britannia, and of the adventures of his children and friends in his discovery and rescue. 170 engravings. 8°. Philadelphia, 1874. 2 copies . . . . 4 . 1235–36

VERSES of many days. W. O. Stoddard. 16°. New York, 1875 . . . 21 . 231

VERY (A) young couple. 16°. New York, 1874 . . . . 4 . 827

VICISSITUDES of Bessie Fairfax. H. Parr. 16°. Philadelphia [n. d.] . 4 . 356

VICTOR'S triumph. E. D. E. N. Southworth. 12°. Philadelphia, 1874 . 4 . 1005

VINCENT, Frank, *jun.* The land of the white elephant: sights in south-eastern Asia. A personal narrative of travel and adventure in Farther India, embracing the countries of Burmah, Siam, Cambodia, and Cochin China, 1871–72. With map, plans, and illustrations. 8°. New York, 1874 . . . . 13 . 1340

VIOLLET-LEDUC, Eugène Emmanuel. The story of (the building of) a house. Trans. from the French by George M. Towle. Illustrated. 8°. Boston, 1874 . . . . 4 . 1301

VIRGINIA, Message of the governor of, and accompanying documents, 1862. 8°. Richmond, 1862 . . . . 13 . 1401

VIVIA. E. D. E. N. Southworth. 12°. Philadelphia, 1857 . . . . . 4 . 1036

VOICE (The) in speaking. *Madame* Emma Seiler. 16°. Philadelphia, 1875. 13 . 1165

VON Siebold, C. Th. Anatomy of the invertebrata. Trans. from the German with additions and notes by Waldo I. Burnett. 8°. Boston, 1874. 13 . 1305

W.

WAGNER, Richard, and the music of the future. Franz Hueffer. 8°. London, 1874 . . . . 13 . 1239

WALDFRIED: a novel. Berthold Auerbach. 12°. New York, 1874 . . . 4 . 805

WALDO, S. Putnam. The tour of James Monroe, President of the United States, in the year 1817, with a sketch of his life. 16°. Hartford, 1818. 13 . 869

WALKER, Francis A. The Indian question. Map. 12°. Boston, 1874. 13 . 857

WALLER, Horace. The last journals of David Livingstone in Central Africa, from 1865 to his death. Continued by a narrative of his last moments and sufferings, obtained from his faithful servants, Chuma and Susi. With portrait, maps, and illustrations. L. 8°. New York, 1875 . . . . 13 . 1310

WALLER, S. E. Six weeks in the saddle: a painter's journal in Iceland. Illustrated. Sm. 8°. London, 1874 . . . . 13 . 121

WALLINGTON, Nehemiah, *compiler*. Historical notices of events occurring chiefly in the reign of Charles I. From the original MSS. with notes and illustrations. 2 v. Sm. 8°. London, 1869 . . . . 13 . 148–9

*WANLEY, Nathan. The wonders of the little world; or, a general history of man. 2 v. 8°. London, 1806 . . . . 13 . 1409–10

WARFIELD, Caroline A. Miriam Montfort. A novel. 12°. New York, 1873 . . . . 4 . 268

WARNER, Susan. [*Elizabeth Wetherell.*] The flag of truce. Illustrated. 16°. New York, 1875 . . . . 4 . 375

Sceptres and crowns. Illustrated. 16°. New York, 1875 . . . . . 4 . 376

WARREN, *Miss*. John Knox and his times. 16°. New York [n. d.] . . 13 . 969
WARREN, Nathan B. The Lady of Lawford, and other Christmas stories. Illustrated. 12°. Troy, 1874 . . . . 4 . 561
WARREN, Samuel. Ten thousand a year. A new edition, carefully revised, with notes and illustrations. 2 v. in 1. Sm. 8°. Edinburgh, 1873 . 4 . 468
WAR-TRAIL (The). M. Reid. 12°. New York, 1874 . . . . 4 . 1262
WASHBURN, Katherine Sedgwick, *formerly Mrs. Valerio*. The Italian girl. 12°. Boston, 1874 . . . . 4 . 479
WATCH and wait. W. T. Adams. 16°. Boston, 1875 . . . . 4 . 334
WATER (The) babies: a fairy tale for a land baby. *Rev.* Charles Kingsley. Sm. 8°. London, 1872 . . . . 4 . 460
WATER-WITCH (The). J. F. Cooper. 12°. New York, 1873 . . . . . 4 . 1067
WATT, James, Origin and progress of the mechanical inventions of. By James P. Muirhead. 3 v. 8°. London, 1854 . . . . 13 . 1227-29
WAVERLEY. *Sir* W. Scott. 2 v. in 1. 12°. Boston, 1874 . . . . . . 4 . 235
WAY (The) of the world. W. T. Adams. 12°. Boston, 1875 . . . . . 4 . 353
WAYS (The) of the hour. J. F. Cooper. 12°. New York, 1873 . . . . 4 . 1068
WEBB, *Mrs.* J. B. Oliver Wyndham; a tale of the great plague. 16°. New York [n. d.] . . . . 4 . 878
*WEBSTER, Daniel, and HAYNE, Robert Young. Speeches in the United States senate, on Mr. Foot's resolution of January, 1830; also Daniel Webster's speech in the senate of the United States, May 7, 1850, on the slavery compromise. 8°. Philadelphia [n. d.] . . . . 13 . 1407
WELLES, Gideon. Lincoln and Seward. Remarks upon the memorial address of Charles Francis Adams, on the late William H. Seward, with incidents and comments illustrative of the measures and policy of the administration of Abraham Lincoln, and views as to the relative positions of the late president and secretary of state. 16°. New York, 1874 . . . . 13 . 163
WEPT (The) of Wish-Ton-Wish. J. F. Cooper. 12°. New York, 1873 . 4 . 1069
WERNER, Ernst. Broken Chains. Trans. from the German, by Frances A. Shaw. 8°. Boston, 1875 . . . . 4 . 523
WEST lawn. M. J. Holmes. 12°. New York, 1874. 2 copies . . . 3 . 1365-66
WESTCOTT, Margaret. Bessie Wilmerton; or, money, and what came of it. 12°. New York, 1874 . . . . 4 . 976
WESTMINSTER hall, Memories of. Edward Foss. 2 v. 8°. New York, 1874 . . . . 13 . 1333-34
* WESTON, W. On the rejection of the Christian miracles by the heathens. 8°. Cambridge, 1746 . . . . 13 . 843
WETHERELL, Elizabeth [*Pseud.*]. *See* WARNER, Susan.
WHALEMAN'S (The) adventures. W. H. Thomes. 12°. Boston, 1875. . 4 . 1136
WHAT might have been expected. F. R. Stockton. 16°. New York, 1874 . . . . 4 . 842
WHAT shall we do to-night? or, social amusements for evening parties. Illustrated. By Leger D. Mayne [*pseud.*]. 12°. New York, 1873 . 13 . 114
WHATELY, Richard. Easy lessons in reasoning. 12°. Boston, 1852 . . 13 . 140
WHICH shall it be? *Mrs.* Alexander. 16°. New York, 1874 . . . . . 4 . 853
WHISPERING (The) pine. E. Kellogg. 16°. Boston, 1875 . . . . . 4 . 955
WHISPERS from fairy land. E. H. Knatchbull-Hugessen. Sm. 8°. New York, 1875 . . . . 4 . 365

WHITE, George S. Memoir of Samuel Slater, the father of American manufactures, connected, with a history of the rise and progress of the cotton manufacture in England and America. With remarks on the moral influence of manufactories in the United States. Illustrated by 30 engravings. 8°. Philadelphia, 1836 . . . . 13 . 1408
WHITE (The) chief. M. Reid. 12°. New York, 1874 . . . . 4 . 1263
WHITE (The) gauntlet. M. Reid. 12°. New York, 1874 . . . . 4 . 1264
WHITE lies. C. Reade. Sm. 8°. Boston, 1872 . . . . 4 . 1130
WHITEHURST, Felix M. Court and social life in France under Napoleon the third. 2 v. 8°. London, 1873. . . . . 13 . 1223-24
WHITNEY, William Dwight. Oriental and linguistic studies. The east and the west, religion and mythology, orthography and phonology, Hindu astronomy. 12°. New York, 1874 . . . . 13 . 1145
WHITTIER, John Greenleaf. Hazel-blossoms. 16°. Boston, 1875 . . . 21 . 243
WHO breaks — pays. *Mrs.* C. Jenkin. 16°. New York, 1873 . . . . 4 . 869
WIDOW (The) and the marquess. T. Hook. 16°. London [n. d.] . . . 4 . 821
WIDOW'S (The) son. E. D. E. N. Southworth. 12°. Philadelphia, 1867 4 . 1037
WIFE'S (The) victory. E. D. E. N. Southworth. 12°. Philadelphia, 1854 4 . 1038
WIKOFF, Henry. The four civilizations of the world; an historical retrospect. 12°. Philadelphia, 1874 . . . . 13 . 170
WILBERFORCE, Henry William. The church and the empires, historical periods. Preceded by a memoir of the author by J. H. Newman. Portrait. 8°. London, 1874 . . . . 13 . 1240
WILD (The) huntress. M. Reid. 12°. New York, 1874 . . . . 4 . 1265
WILD life. M. Reid. 12°. New York, 1874 . . . . 4 . 1266
WILD (The) man of the west. R. M. Ballantyne. 16°. Philadelphia [n. d.]. 4 . 1210
WILD (The) north land. W. F. Butler. 8°. London, 1874 . . . . . . 13 . 1156
WILKINSON, William Cleaver. A free lance in the field of life and letters. 12°. New York, 1874 . . . . 13 . 1168
WILL Adams, the first Englishman in Japan. W. Dalton. Sm. 8°. London [n. d.] . . . . 4 . 571
WILSON, Henry. History of the rise and fall of the slave power in America. 2 v. Roy. 8°. Boston, 1875 . . . . 13 . 1414-15
WILSON, James Grant. Sketches of illustrious soldiers. With engravings and autographs. 12°. New York, 1874 . . . . 13 . 954
WINCHELL, Alexander. The doctrine of evolution: its data, its principles, its speculations, and its theistic bearings. 16°. New York, 1874 . 13 . 172
WINDSOR Castle. An historical romance. W. H. Ainsworth. 16°. London [n. d.] . . . . 4 . 1183
WING-AND-WING. J. F. Cooper. 12°. New York, 1873 . . . . . . 4 . 1070
WINNING his spurs. E. Kellogg. 16°. Boston, 1875 . . . . 4 . 956
WINSCOM, Jane Anne. Onward; or, the mountain clamberers. A tale of progress. 16°. New York [n. d.] . . . . 4 . 439
WINTER (The) fire. *A sequel* to "Summer driftwood." Rose Porter. 16°. New York, 1874 . . . . 4 . 829
WINTER homes for invalids. J. W. Howe. Sm. 8°. New York, 1875 . 13 . 941
WITHROW, William Henry. The catacombs of Rome, and their testimony relative to primitive Christianity. Illustrated. Sm. 8°. New York, 1874. 13 . 1141

Note. — This book is a popular summary of present knowledge on this subject: it is illustrated by frequent pagan sepulchral inscriptions,

WITHROW, William Henry. *Note (continued).*

and by citations from the writings of the fathers, which often throw much light on the condition of early Christian society. There are many hundreds of early Christian inscriptions carefully translated; a very large proportion of which have never before appeared in English. A general survey of the whole subject as a starting point for further study can be found in McClintock and Strong's Cyclopædia with references, vol. ii. p. 145 [2 . 629], and in Murray's handbook of Rome [13 . 1176]. Also see Harper's monthly, vol. x. [20 . 510]; Edinburgh review, vol. 109, p. 86 [15 . 135]; and vol. 120, p. 217 [15 . 147]. See a chapter in Castelar's "Old Rome and New Italy" [13 . 1270], and in Francis Wey's "Rome." [3 . 602].

*WOLF, Joseph. The life and habits of wild animals, with descriptive letter-press by Daniel Giraud Elliot. Illustrations. 4°. New York, 1874 . . . . 13 . 1501

WOMAN before the law. J. Proffatt. 16°. New York, 1874 . . . . . . 13 . 1160

WOMAN in the nineteenth century. S. M. F. Ossoli. 12°. Boston, 1874 . 13 . 129

WOMEN (The) of the Arabs. Rev. H. H. Jessup. 12°. New York, 1873. 13 . 125

*WONDERS of the little world. N. Wanley. 2 v. 8°. London, 1806. 13 . 1409–10

WONDERFUL (A) woman. M. A. Fleming. 12°. New York, 1874. . . . 4 . 1336

WOOD, John George. Trespassers, showing how the inhabitants of earth, air, and water are enabled to trespass on domains not their own. Illustrated. Sq. 8°. New York [n. d.] . . . . 13 . 1133

WOOD, *Lady*. Sabina. A novel. 16°. London, 1869. 2 copies . . . 4 . 847–8

WOOD-RANGERS (The). M. Reid. 12°. New York, 1874 . . . . 4 . 1267

WOODRUFF, Julia Louisa Matilda. [*W. M. L. Jay.*] Holden with the cords. 12°. New York, 1874 . . . . 4 . 451

WOODSTOCK. *Sir* W. Scott. 2 v. in 1. 12°. Boston, 1872 . . . . . . 4 . 236

WOODVILLE, Jennie [*Pseud.*]. Edith's mistake; or, left to herself. Fiction. 16°. Philadelphia, 1874 . . . . 4 . 979

WOOING (The) o't. *Mrs.* Alexander. 16°. New York, 1873 . . . . . . 4 . 854

WOOLSEY, Sarah Chauncey. [*Susan Coolidge.*] Mischief's Thanksgiving, and other (juvenile) stories. Illustrated. 16°. Boston, 1874. . . . 4 . 570

WOOLSON, Abba Goold, *editor.* Dress-reform: a series of lectures delivered in Boston, on dress as it affects the health of woman. Illustrations. 16°. Boston, 1874 . . . . 13 . 963

*WOOSTER, David, *editor.* Alpine plants: figures and descriptions of some of the most striking and beautiful Alpine flowers. 8°. London, 1874. . . . . 13 . 1542

*WORCESTER, Mass. Atlas of the city of, from surveys by F. W. Beers, G. P. Sanford, and others. Roy. 4°. New York, 1870 . . . . . . 15 . 1421

*Atlas of the county of. From surveys by F. W. Beers, G. P. Sanford, and others. Roy. 4°. New York, 1870 . . . . 15 . 1422

WORDSWORTH, Dorothy. Recollections of a tour made [with Coleridge and W. Wordsworth] in Scotland, A. D. 1803. Edited by J. C. Shairp. Sm. 8°. New York, 1874. . . . . 13 . 955

WORDSWORTH, Shelley, Keats, and other essays. D. Masson. Sm. 8°. London, 1874 . . . . 13 . 105

WORK and win. W. T. Adams. 16°. Boston, 1875 . . . . 4 . 335

WORKING to win. Maggie Symington. 12°. New York [n. d.]. . . . 4 . 459

WORKINGMEN'S homes. Essays and stories. E. E. Hale *and others.* 16°. Boston, 1874. . . . . 13 . 177

WORKS of W. E. Channing. 6 v. 12°. Boston, 1848 . . . . 13 . 832–37

WORKS of George Chapman. Edited with notes by R. H. Shepard. Sm. 8°. London, 1874 . . . . 21 . 227
*WORKS of James Gillray, the caricaturist; with the history of his life and times. With over four hundred illustrations. Edited by Thomas Wright. Roy. 4°. London [n. d.]. . . . . 13 . 1515
*WORKS of Peter Pindar, with some account of his life. 4 v. 24°. London, 1816 . . . . 21 . 256–59
WORKS of Richard Brinsley Sheridan. Edited by E. Stainforth. Sm. 8°. London, 1874. . . . . 21 . 225
WORKS of Charles Sumner. Vols. 8 and 9. 8°. Boston, 1873–74. . 13 . 1246–47
WORLD (The) on wheels. B. F. Taylor. Sm. 8°. Chicago, 1874 . . . 4 . 262
*WOTTON, *Sir* Henry. Reliquiæ Wottonianæ; or, a collection of lives, letters, and poems, with characters of sundry personages; and other incomparable pieces of language and art. Sm. 8°. London, 1651 . 13 . 891
WRECKED on a reef; or, twenty months among the Auckland isles. From the French of F. E. Raynal. Sm. 8°. London, 1874 . . . . . 4 . 263
WRECKMASTER (The). Knickerbocker, jun. [*Pseud.*]. 16°. Philadelphia, 1870 . . . . 4 . 939
WRIGHT, Daniel Thew. Mrs. Armington's ward; or, the inferior sex. 16°. Boston, 1874 . . . . 4 . 837
*WRIGHT, Thomas, *editor*. The works of James Gillray, the caricaturist; with the history of his life and times. With over 400 illustrations. Roy. 4°. London [n. d.] . . . . 13 . 1515
WRINKLES; or, hints to sportsmen. H. A. Lloyd. Sm. 8°. London, 1874. 4 . 476
WYANDOTTE. J. F. Cooper. 12°. New York, 1873 . . . . 4 .1071

Y.

YACHT (The) club. W. T. Adams. 16°. Boston, 1874 . . . . 4 . 339
YALE lectures on preaching. H. W. Beecher. Third series. Sm. 8°. New York, 1874 . . . . 13 . 157
YANKEE (The) middy. W. T. Adams. 16°. Boston, 1875 . . . . . 4 . 306
YATES, Edmund. A dangerous game. 8°. Boston, 1874 . . . . 4 . 530
YOUNG, Charles F. T. Fires, fire engines, and fire brigades, with a history of manual and steam fire engines. 8°. London, 1866 . . . . . . 13 . 1061
YOUNG (The) deliverers of Pleasant Cove. E. Kellogg. 16°. Boston, 1874 . . . . 4 . 948
YOUNG (The) fur traders. R. M. Ballantyne. Sm. 8°. Edinburgh, 1856. 4 . 1211
YOUNG (The) lieutenant. W. T. Adams. 16°. Boston, 1875 . . . . 4 . 303
YOUNG (The) moose hunters. C. A. Stephens. Sm. 8°. Boston, 1874. 2 copies . . . . 4 . 909–10
YOUNG (The) ship-builders of Elm Island. E. Kellogg. 16°. Boston, 1875. 4 . 944
YOUNG Singleton. Talbot Gwynne. 16°. London [n. d.] . . . . . 4 . 845
YOUNG (The) voyageurs. M. Reid. 16°. Boston, 1874 . . . . 4 . 1268
YOUNG (The) whaler. F. Gerstaecker. 16°. London [n. d.]. . . . . 4 . 380
YOUNG (The) yägers. M. Reid. 16°. Boston, 1874 . . . . 4 . 1269

Z.

ZELDA's fortune. R. E. Francillon. 8°. Boston, 1874 . . . . 4 . 531

ZINCKE, Foster-Barham. Egypt of the Pharaohs and of the Kedivé. 8°. London, 1873 . . . . 13 . 1352

Swiss allmends, and a walk to see them; being a second month in Switzerland. Folded map. Sm. 8°. London, 1874 . . . . . . 13 . 953

Note. — "Allmend" means "land held and used in common." With this volume is a good map, giving the roads, railways, mountains, and glaciers, both of Switzerland and of the contiguous region of France and Italy.

www.ingramcontent.com/pod-product-compliance
Lightning Source LLC
Chambersburg PA
CBHW031440270326
41930CB00007B/800
9783337234171